First published in March 2006

by Makar Press, Troon
www.makarpress.co.uk

Lottery Grants for Local Groups
AWARDS FOR ALL

Ayr Writers' Club acknowledges the support of National Lottery Awards for All towards the publication of this book.

British Library Cataloguing in Publication Data
A catalogue record for this book is available from the British Library.

ISBN 0-9547084-5-8
ISBN 978-0-9547084-5-8

Printed by Core Image, East Kilbride

800 Words

Poetry and Prose to mark
800 years of Ayr's Royal Charter

Ayr Writers' Club

Edited by Ann Burnett and Rowena M Love

Contents

Acknowledgements 6
Debby Broughton-Hay *Foreword* 7
Joanne Harris *Short Story Adjudication* 8
Dr. E. J. Yeaman *Verdant Boughs at Twilight* 10
Rowena M Love *The Dolphin* 16
Marion Montgomery *Voyage to Corrievreckan* 18
Janice Johnston *How to Wash a Car* 19
Douglas Gray *Cupid Complaining to Venus (c. 1530)* 24
Ann Burnett *Dancin at Whitecraigs* 26
Jim Hughes *Comma* 31
Kate Ayres *The Cry* 32
Sheila Templeton *A Bonnie Fechter* 36
Janice Johnston *Keeping Promises* 38
Norman Bissett *Portrait of a Lady* 41
Michael Malone *Drinking Jesus' Blood* 42
Des Dillon *He Ain't Heavy* 44
Marion Montgomery *Andrew* 49

Rowena M Love *Song of Wallace* **50**
Marion Reid *The Towering Wallace* **51**
Fiona Atchison *Tongue-Tied* **52**
Sylvia Cohen *Behind a Suburban Street* **60**
Maya Rae McLaughlin *Obeahman* **62**
Knotbrook Taylor *island man does a Dylan* **66**
Janice Johnston *Bridges* **68**
Ann Burnett *Jean Armour Speaks* **71**
Rowena M Love *Dear Diaries* **72**
Douglas Gray *Intimates* **77**
Norman Bissett *In the Gorbals* **78**
Ann Burnett *Knitting for Joyce* **80**
Rowena M Love *The Ben* **85**
Duncan Fraser *Other* **86**
Sheila Grant *Ayr Writers' Club* **88**
Biographies **90**

Acknowledgements

Ayr Writers' Club wish to acknowledge the support of the National Lottery Awards for All towards the Ayr 800 National Short Story and Poetry Competition, the one day Creative Writing Event and the production of this anthology.

The Club would also like to thank all those involved in the running of both the conference and the competition. In particular, Debby Broughton-Hay, who put in a huge amount of effort to ensure their success.

Acknowledgement is also given to the following publications:

- Reach Poetry Magazine and The Chameleon of Happiness (published by Makar Press, 2004) for *The Dolphin.*
- Poetry Scotland (issue 38) for *Voyage to Corrievreckan.*
- New Writing Scotland 17, Friends and Kangaroos (published by ASLS, 1999) for *Comma.*
- The Herald for *A Bonnie Fechter*, on the occasion of its being awarded second prize in the McCash Prize for Scots Poetry run jointly by the Herald and Glasgow University.
- In the Raw (published by Makar Press, 2004) for *Drinking Jesus' Blood.*
- Saints: A Visual Guide by E Mornin (published by Novalis, 2006) for *Andrew*
- The Wallace Muse edited by Lesley Duncan and Elspeth King (published by Luath Press, 2005) for *Song of Wallace* and *The Towering Wallace.*
- The Scots Magazine (July 2005) for *The Ben.*

Foreword

DEBBY BROUGHTON-HAY

In 2005, the town of Ayr celebrated its 800th anniversary and to mark this, there was a year-long series of events put together by a wide range of clubs and groups throughout the town. For our part, members from Ayr Writers' Club decided to organise a National Short Story and Poetry Competition and also a one-day Creative Writing event. In this book, you will find the winning entries from both competitions along with some of the Highly Commended poetry. In addition, we have included a selection of prize-winning and published work from club members and also submissions from some of the established writers who have been involved with the club during this venture.

This Anthology is the culmination of a two-year project that has involved a great many people who are due our thanks. Firstly, Ayr Writers' Club which brought us all together, the Ayr Guildry whose 800-year celebrations sparked the idea and the Lottery Awards For All Fund for providing financial support. Thanks also to the participants, the more than 250 entrants of our Short Story and Poetry Competitions and delegates of our Creative Writing Day in October 2005. Lastly, the speakers from that writing event who inspired and encouraged us, Des Dillon, Janice Galloway and Jenny Colgan. Thank you also to Joanne Harris who judged our Short Story Competition and the poets of the Makar Press (Jim Hughes, Rowena M Love, Michael Malone and Sheila Templeton) who judged the poetry.

I hope the reading of this book gives you as much pleasure as the creating of it did for us.

President, Ayr Writers' Club
January 2006

Adjudication

Joanne Harris

I really enjoyed reading the stories, they were all of very high quality and there was a nice breadth of variety.

Basically, what I have judged on is originality of thought, proficiency of style and the quality of plotting and construction. I found the last bit has tested some of the writers, as some of the pieces, although very fine pieces of writing in themselves, didn't quite cut it as stories. Some were pieces of mood writing rather than actual stories with development of plot.

According to my criteria, therefore, I wasn't able to rate some of the stories as highly as perhaps the writing deserved. This tends to be a problem with short stories generally and not just the entries to this competition and this is why the ones I have chosen, although there may be stylistic flaws in some, have been chosen.

The three winners:

1. Verdant Boughs at Twilight. I really liked this one. It was an original thought, very nice, clear, well written snappy dialogue and very funny. Terrific.

2. The Cry. Nice opening paragraph. Good impact, genuinely intriguing. Concise and clear. Very good indeed.

3. Obeahman. This one is nicely paced, well constructed with a good sense of place and atmosphere and a tremendous

use of humour. Stylistically it could be polished as there is an excessive number of adjectives and adverbs but it is still very good and deserves a mention.

Congratulations to all the entrants and thanks to the Ayr Writers' Club for giving me the opportunity to read the stories. I have enjoyed being involved with the competition.

With best wishes,

Joanne Harris

When it came to the Ayr 800 Poetry Competition, the Makar Press poets awarded a first, second and third prize. They also identified Highly Commended and Commended poems. This collection includes all of the prize winning and Highly Commended poems.

1st – Cupid Complaining to Venus (c. 1530)
2nd – Portrait of a Lady
3rd – island man does a Dylan

Highly Commended:
Behind a Suburban Street
In the Gorbals
Other
Intimates

Verdant Boughs at Twilight

DR. E. J. YEAMAN

'What shall I try now? Hell, it doesn't matter. I'll punch a few buttons and see what I get.'

'Good morning. *Verdant Boughs at Twilight.* Butler (page 171) speaking.'

'Eh? What's that?'

'*Verdant Boughs at Twilight.* Butler (page 171) speaking. May I assist you, sir?'

'Assist me? Well, you might start by explaining that *Verdant Boughs at Twilight* stuff.'

'Yes, sir. You have dialled the line for *Verdant Boughs at Twilight.*'

'Now, could you translate that for me? Into English, preferably.'

'I suspect that I perceive the reason for this misunderstanding. May I enquire how you came to dial this number, sir?'

'Well, if you must know, I was bored, so I just dialled a number, any old number. I know it sounds bloody stupid, but… it was like a lucky dip. I hoped I might find somebody interesting.'

'Indeed, sir. I suspected as much. You have unwittingly dialled a fiction line.'

'A fiction line?'

'Yes, sir. This is the residence of all the characters in the novel, *Verdant Boughs at Twilight*, written by Artemis Brocklebank in 1891.'

'You're joking!'

'No, I assure you, sir. Every extant work of fiction is on the telephone. You might have reached someone from *The Old Curiosity Shop*, or *Noddy in Toyland*, or *Titanic*. You simply happened to dial the number of *Verdant Boughs at Twilight*.'

'That's bloody amazing! So you're only a character in a novel? You don't really exist.'

'I would beg to differ with you there, sir. As long as at least one copy of the novel in question exists, and as long as there is someone to read it, then we can live – live in a reader's imagination.'

'But you don't really live in… in fact?'

'That is a matter of opinion, sir. Granted, I do not live in the same plane of existence as you do. We can never meet, but we can converse over the telephone – as you have discovered, sir.'

'I just don't believe it!'

'I can assure you, sir, that everything is just as I have described. The situation is well known in the world of fiction, but not, apparently, to you, sir.'

'Not to me! I just don't believe it!'

'I am sorry, sir, but I can only repeat the assurance…'

'No. I'm sorry. I'm sorry. I wasn't doubting you. It's just… the idea takes a lot of getting used to. So you're a character in a book?'

'Yes, sir. *Verdant Boughs at Twilight*, by Artemis Brocklebank.'

'I've never heard of it.'

'No. I fear that it is not considered one of the classics of literature.'

'And what's your name?'

'I have no name, sir. Mr Brocklebank never troubled to furnish me with a name. I am simply designated, "Butler (page 171)".'

'Page 171?'

'Yes, sir. Mr Brocklebank was rather liberal with butlers in Verdant Boughs at Twilight. There are five stately homes in the story, and each of them has a butler – at least one butler. I am designated "Butler (page171)" to distinguish me from the seven other un-named butlers who appear in the work. There's "Butler (page 32)", "Butler (page 100)", "Butler (page 163)", "Butler…"'

'Yes, I get the idea. This is amazing! What do you look like?'

'Why, sir, I look like a butler.'

'But what does that mean? How old are you? How are you dressed?'

'You must be the judge of that, sir. Mr Brocklebank did not specify any details of my age or appearance, so these are left to the imagination of the reader.'

'So if I imagine you as a fat slob with a blotchy red nose and flat feet, then that's what you'd become?'

'I beg you sir, don't. I trust that I have given you no offence which would cause you to treat me in such a manner.'

'No, of course not. I see you as well-dressed and dignified. What do you do in the book anyway?'

'I draw open the great double doors of Verdant Boughs, and…'

'Verdant Boughs?'

'Yes, sir. Verdant Boughs is the name of Lord Tillingham's country seat. I welcome the Lady Patricia Laverock with the words, "Good afternoon, my lady" and conduct her to the drawing room where Lord Tillingham awaits.'

'Is that it?'

'Is that what, sir?'

'Is that all you do in the book?'

'Yes, sir. There was some debate over my identity with a butler who draws open the great double doors of Verdant Boughs on page 389 and welcomes Lady Patricia, but that individual greets her with the words, "Good afternoon, your ladyship" so, after enquiry, the identity was not established and we are regarded as two different characters.'

'I know! You're Mr Mischief!'

'Mr Mischief, sir?'

'Yes, the guy on that radio show – what's it called? – the Gary Green Show. You know – the guy that makes these hoax phone calls. You're Mr Mischief!'

'I can assure you, sir, that I am **not** Mr Mischief. I believe that I have heard of the individual to whom you allude, and I can only protest – most strongly – that I am **not** Mr Mischief.'

'But when did you tell me your book was written?'

'1891, sir.'

'Well, tell me this. How do you know about this year's radio show? Radio wasn't even invented in 1891. Got you there, eh!'

'Oh, but we can receive current radio transmissions, sir. And television. I believe that, if you would care, I could find you the telephone number of *Neighbours*. Or *Coronation Street*.'

'No. Nonono! I'll take your word for it. Go on telling me about yourself. You don't sound very important.'

'Important! Of course my role is important, if I may be as bold as to say so, sir. It is minor. I grant you that. But it is not unimportant. If I did not feature in the story, then there would be no one to draw open the great double doors of Verdant Boughs and escort Lady Patricia to meet Lord Tillingham.'

'And that would be bad?'

'That would be extremely bad, sir. On that meeting hinges the remainder of the narrative. If Lady Patricia did not meet Lord Tillingham, she could not explain how her daughter Penelope had visited… Go away!'

'Eh?'

'Go away, you two! Go to your room! I will deal with you later!'

'What the hell are you talking about?'

'I do apologise, sir. These were the two ragged urchins who steal Penelope's parasol on page 211. They frequently find their way in here, causing trouble.'

'Bloody Hell! Your novel seems to have quite a gang of characters.'

'Indeed it does, sir. Mr Brocklebank appears to have relished painting a broad canvas. He was generous in his creation of characters. There are four hundred and seventeen of us.'

'Four hundred and seventeen! Where on earth – or elsewhere – do you all live?'

'We reside in a huge mansion – called Verdant Boughs of course.'

'That sounds very posh.'

'It is… elegant, sir. The house is very well appointed. It is meticulously described in *Verdant Boughs at Twilight.* But the catering, I fear, does not match the appearance.'

'Catering? You must have housekeepers, cooks and so on to run the place.'

'No, sir. No doubt Mr Brocklebank in his wisdom assumed that there were such persons on the premises but unfortunately he neglected to mention them in the story, so they cannot exist.'

'So what do you do?'

'We must do the best we can, sir. Fortunately, several gardeners are mentioned in the text, and a crowd of simple villagers, and they all do their share of cooking and cleaning. Even Lady Patricia helps when we can persuade her that she is simply a character like the rest of us.'

'But can't you import some maids and housekeepers?'

'From where, sir?'

'From other stories.'

'Oh, no, sir. Every book, every story, is strictly self-contained. We are not permitted to mingle with the characters from any other story.'

'So you're stuck in that one place, that one Verdant Boughs, with four hundred and sixteen other characters?'

'That is so, sir.'

'What about characters that appear in more than one book?'

'They are permitted to wander among the scenarios of the books in which they appear. I am pleased to notice that that will apply to me now.'

'To you? How?'

'Well, sir, I appear in the original story, *Verdant Boughs at Twilight*. But now I also appear in this story, the story of our telephone conversation. I suspect that I shall mainly reside, as I have done, in *Verdant Boughs*. But, whenever I feel like a spot of peace and quiet, I shall look forward to paying you a visit in your little cottage.'

'Me! In my little cottage?'

'Yes, sir. This story is so short and it has so few characters that it will not merit anything larger than a two-roomed cottage.'

'What! Am I doomed to spend my existence in a two-roomed cottage, with only you popping in occasionally?'

'Yes, sir. After all, there need only be sufficient room for you, and me – oh, and the two ragged urchins.'

'The two ragged urchins!'

'Yes, sir. Remember, they feature in this story, as well as Mr Brocklebank's *Verdant Boughs at Twilight*. They'll be free to visit you as they please.'

'What!'

'I fear so, sir, and there is nothing we can do about it. That's the way the system operates. Well, sir, it has been very pleasant talking to you. I look forward to meeting you in the near future. So farewell, or perhaps I may be permitted to say, *au revoir*.'

'Hang on, hang on, butler. This story is not finished yet, is it?'

'No, sir.'

'Then I'll tell you about my neighbours. One is a nice old dear, an old teacher who likes nothing better than looking after ragged urchins and keeping them in order. You see what I mean?'

'Yes, sir. Indeed I do. And you won't forget your other neighbour, the buxom, good-natured housekeeper, who's an excellent cook?'

'I'm glad you mentioned her, butler. And I mustn't forget the ten gorgeous girls who live two doors along. They're **very** obliging. And the off-licence down the road. Hey! I think I'm starting to enjoy this story!'

The Dolphin

Rowena M Love

for Insa

Cancer's a queer fish:
anaemic amoeba endlessly mutating;
puffer-fish growths bloated with poison;
or shoals of cells
that prowl like piranhas
stripping my health in their feeding frenzy.

But attitude can attack back,
till I'm the dolphin swimming free
from this sea
of sickness.

I'll trawl my system,
catching cancers and fears,
netting them to wriggle and squirm:
powerless.

I'm the dolphin swimming free.

Modern medicine may have me filleted,
canned and processed,
pumped full of additives –
but the rest is up to me...

I'm the dolphin swimming free.

Dread might dorsal my spine,
tears flood my face with brine
but I... CAN... DO... THIS...

I <u>am</u> the dolphin swimming free.

Voyage to Corrievreckan

MARION MONTGOMERY

No colour this cool dawn in sea or skies.
Engulfed in simple light, the Small Isles gleam
Like pebbles in a bowl of polished steel.
Dark shades seep in. Massed clouds grow purple.
Gold blades of sunshine stab them through
To glance off water, green below our keel,
Where Barnhill's image hangs unrippled.
In this glass Orwell saw the world turned turtle.
There wrote of Peace and Truth which deal
In War and Lies.
When Corrievreckan's growl
Sounds near, we climb ashore, afraid to feel
The power that sucked down Breacan's boat,
Betrayed by brittle hemp, by wool, and tainted hair.
Fear made one faithless girl conceal her shame
But dying Orwell sailed the whirlpool unafraid
And told the truth.

According to legend, Prince Breacan of Norway had to anchor his ship in the whirlpool for three days in order to win the hand of his princess. When the third rope failed, he was sucked down into the whirlpool which became known as 'Breacan's Cauldron' or Corrievreckan.

Barnhill was the house where George Orwell lived while writing 1984.

How to Wash a Car

JANICE JOHNSTON

Matthew sighed and glanced at the clock on the wall. He thought not – 9:15 and he hadn't finished the crossword. The 12-letter, 9 across had proved totally elusive. Or perhaps it was the date – Christopher's birthday – that blocked his concentration. He angled the picture on the table slightly so he could see it better. A neighbour, trying out a new camera, had snapped Christopher another Saturday morning a long time ago, sponge in hand.

He folded the paper precisely and placed it in the rack. Perhaps he'd finish the crossword later, now it was time to wash the car.

'Jenny's or Dino's?'

The lump in the other sleeping bag didn't move. Jake watched the sun rise through the uncurtained window. As shadows slid down the wall, he stretched out his fingers, touching the warmth. His hand closed over a trainer. Weighing it in his hand, he flung it across the room. 'Oy, Sleeping effin' Beauty, Jenny's or Dino's?'

Toffer turned over and sighed loudly. 'Jenny's. She does the best bacon butties.' He rubbed his eyes and yawned. 'I fancy a bacon butty this morning.'

'Christ, Toff,' Jake groaned. 'She'll make us clean all of those huge windows before we get anything.'

'It'll be worth it.' Toffer slipped out of his sleeping bag, still only half awake, and pulled on his clothes, 'C'mon.'

Last night Matthew had parked the Laguna halfway down the drive. Now he could see it was perfectly placed in the centre of the patch of shade created by the house. The car would be cool. When the surface is hot, soapsuds dry faster than they can be rinsed off and they will mark the car, as he'd always told Christopher.

Matthew fixed the hose to a tap and sprayed the surface of the car with a gentle stream. He concentrated on removing the worst of the grime. Mud dripped from the wheel wells on to the concrete below. Matthew remembered Christopher using the hose. He liked to aim the spray into the wheel wells, shooting darts of dirt out and over the wings. Matthew had always chastised him for this. A fine spray from the hose blew back on to Matthew, misting his glasses and forming soft tears on his cheeks.

He sprayed tyre cleaner on the wheels, then measured exactly two capfuls of liquid and poured it into the brown pail with warm water. The scent of lemons, hot soapy lemons, assailed his nostrils. He filled a second pail with clean warm water and carried both outside. This was how Matthew had taught Christopher to wash a car.

'You've missed a bit – top left-hand corner.' Jenny held on to the plate. A customer at another table hollered for attention but she ignored him.

Toffer grinned. 'Jake's side – sheer laziness. I'll dock his pay.' He grabbed a butty and took a bite. 'Mmm, manna from heaven, and tea – nectar of the Gods.'

Jenny laughed, 'You are a strange lad, Toffer, you and your sayings.' She ruffled his untidy blond hair and headed back to the counter.

Jake shook his head. 'They always want to mother you.'

'Don't complain.' Toffer licked brown sauce from his lips and picked up a fork. 'She gave us scrambled eggs, too.'

The sponge fitted perfectly into Matthew's hand. He dunked it into the soapy water and quickly brought it to the roof of the car. He moved the sponge in wide swirls, covering the whole area, then rinsed it off in the pail of plain water. This allowed any gravel or grit caught in the sponge to be washed out, preventing it from scratching the car's surface. Once he finished the roof, he moved on to the windshield. The wipers stubbornly clung to the glass before yielding to his hand. He pulled the soapy sponge up the wiper blade, removing any dirt and feeling for nicks or cuts in the rubber. He rinsed and soaked the sponge again before rubbing it into every corner of the glass, then swirling it over the bonnet. The back window, spoiler and boot were treated with the same care. Matthew had tried to instil in Christopher the importance of doing a job properly. He emptied out the dirty water. A narrow stream flowed down the drive and on to the tarmac of the road. Matthew turned on the hose and began to rinse off the top of the car.

'You'd save yourself a fortune if you used the supermarket stuff.' Jake squeezed a green stream into his bucket of water.

'Nah, that stuff takes the top coat off the car's finish.' Toffer pulled a bottle from his pocket, poured two capfuls into his pail, then shoved it back in his jacket. He swirled the water with his squeegee and breathed in the tangy scent of soapy lemons.

'Why do you care? Three quarters of the bastards don't pay us anyway.' Jake thumped his pail down at their usual traffic lights. Water slopped over the edge of the bucket.

Toffer followed. 'Yeah, but some do pay – and they pay more if we do a decent job.'

'But they haven't a clue what's in the water.'

'No – but I do.' Toffer placed his bucket on the ground and sat on the barrier beside Jake.

Before filling the pails with more water, Matthew picked up a soft brush and began cleaning the tyre rims and wheel covers. He took his time, methodically brushing every crevice. His knees ached, crouching in such an awkward position.

The next set of pails was used to wash the driver's side. He made sure to push the sponge into each indentation for the door handles. The corner of every window and the wing mirror demanded special attention. Matthew couldn't abide a curve of dirt at the corner. Sheer laziness, he'd told Christopher.

Again, he rinsed all the suds off with the hose before refilling the pails. He washed the passenger side, taking the same care with the windows, wing mirror and handle indentations. If a job's worth doing, it's worth doing well, he could hear himself telling Christopher.

'Here we go. Mini or Escort?' Jake grabbed his squeegee.

'The woman.' Toffer moved towards the Mini and began to wash the windscreen, making sure to push the sponge into every corner then pulling the squeegee smartly across to rinse the suds away.

He smiled and laughed as the driver handed over some change.

'You always pick the payers.' Jake slouched on the barrier. 'That bastard in the Escort started his wipers and gave me the finger before I even stepped off the pavement.'

The front bumper took more time. It was caked with mud and the lights and number plate had attracted bugs. Matthew soaked, rubbed and rinsed repeatedly, removing every last trace of the previous week's journeys.

It had been much quicker when Christopher had been there to help, Matthew thought. They had been a good team, once Matthew had trained him in the best way to wash a car.

The rear bumper was next. He took care sponging the number plate. A sharp corner had caught Christopher's arm one time, leaving a nasty scar when he'd pulled back. Matthew had renewed the car since then but he'd bought the same make in the same colour, of course.

'Red or silver?'

'Red.' Toffer grabbed his squeegee. He heard the whine of the window as he reached the car.

'Sorry, mate,' the driver said. 'I don't have any change.'

'That's O.K,' Toffer grinned. 'I'll do you a freebie.' He took the same care with this one as he'd taken with every other windscreen he'd done that morning. He pulled the last of the water off with a flourish and slapped the roof, before walking back to the barrier.

Matthew turned on the hose for a final all over rinse. The spray of water sparkled in the sun as the patch of shadow grew smaller. The car shone like a sleek dolphin. Matthew sighed, that had been Christopher's flowery imagery.

He produced some towelling and began to dry the bodywork methodically, starting with the roof then working his way down the bodywork. He emptied the pails and rinsed them with the hose. He used the damp towels to dry them, then piled in the cleaning materials ready for next week. The towels, he placed in the washing machine.

Walking through to the living room, Matthew looked at Christopher's photo once more. He sighed. Christopher had struggled with Matthew's teachings. Perhaps he had been too dogmatic, Matthew thought, as he rolled down his shirtsleeves and straightened his shirt. He walked out to the car, pressed the button on the remote control card and waited for the 'plip' before opening the door. Settling himself in the seat, he adjusted the music from a CD to Radio 4 and reversed out, on to the road.

Jake eyed the lights as another car approached. 'Just the one this time. You or me?'

Toffer glanced at the sleek grey car and absentmindedly rubbed the old scar on his arm. 'You take it. I don't do Lagunas any more.'

Cupid Complaining to Venus (c. 1530)

DOUGLAS GRAY

Lucas Crannach (1472-1553)

The National Gallery, London

Hey, ma, I've been stung by a bee!
The boy begins to wail, honeycomb in hand,
a theft he holds as if it was a heart.
He delegates with brat-like appeal,
staring at her flashy orange hat,
whose satellites of pompom form a halo.

At the height of her knee indignant,
she calmly turns away, kind of smug
and wears a musing smile— not much more
on gracile flesh, a heavy necklace weave,
arm aloft without a hint of hair.

A leg is raised, the toes are spread,
the mound is slyly hidden, a tree
is ripe with fruit above her head.
She's pulling on a bough, stood astride
a shadow; for 'ma', in desperate times
like these, will tend to take control:

Oh, my darling angel, there's nothing I can do,
and tempers him with moral-laden words:
If you cannot stand the heat, wee man,
then stay out of the kitchen,
you're quite the little sadist, don't you know;
the skin may be on fire, but see I got an itch,
a bugger of a headache coming on—

these ain't no child-bearing hips,
my breasts don't hang and sway,
but I got legs of the Patron Saint of Luurrve.
There's a guy who's on a promise
and he won't consider no, so how can I
apply myself to consummate seduction?
Do us both a favour, kid, go and string your bow.

Dancin at Whitecraigs

ANN BURNETT

Ma mammy was that pleased when I tellt her I was going to the dancin with some of my pals. Going up to the posh dancin at Whitecraigs.

Ma first dance. The lassies I was going with, Pauline and Sheena, weren't ma regular pals. I'd taken different subjects from them in fourth year. It was hard at first but I stuck in there and kept talking to Sheena and Pauline in classes and eventually they talked to me and let me join their group for experiments and that. I knew they were the popular ones in the class and as I didnae want to be stuck with the odd balls like Ian Hubble, Soapy Bubble he was called, I made sure I got in tow with Pauline and Sheena. And they went to the dance at Whitecraigs every week.

So I knew I'd have to go too if I wantit to be part of their group. It was the Monday period two when Pauline and Sheena were whispering aboot their lumbers from the Saturday while Miss Johnston was fiddling aboot with her chemicals and bunsens.

Sheena and me were listening to Pauline telling all aboot this absolutely dishy guy with a car she'd met. It was a white convertible and he'd driven her home with the hood doon even though it was bliddy freezing and her beehive was just about blown aff her heid. He was at Allan Glen's and had just passed his test in daddy's car and didnae think much of it when Pauline got him to stop ootside her close but he liked her better after she'd stuck her tongue doon his throat and wriggled it aboot a bit. He'd even said he'd see her at Whitecraigs the next week. So that's when I found ma mooth opening and me asking if I could come with them to the dancin. I wantit tae see whit this guy was like.

Miss Johnston finally got her experiment set up then so I didnae get an answer until the break when Pauline said ok I could come with them so long as I didnae hing on to them all the time and I could meet them at the bus stop at seven o'clock.

Ma mammy was fair chuffed when I tellt her. I could see she was thinking back to her youth when she went to dances and got lumbers and I knew I couldnae disappoint her. So I made oot I was dead keen though ma stomach was louping all over the place and it was only Monday. But by the Saturday I was reconciled to ma fate, as Miss McClure, the English teacher, said when she was doing Hamlet with us. She also tellt Sheena and Soapy Bubble to stop having social intercourse across the passage when they were talking. Sheena was jist telling Soapy she'd tell Miss McClure he'd farted if he let on she had her Latin roots book open on her knee when we were doing the weekly test.

On Saturday, ma mind wisnae on the cabbages and that at Littlewoods. I've got a Saturday job in the fruit and veg bit there. I was trying to save up for a new transistor radio so's I could hear Radio Luxemburg wi'oot all the crackling on the auld yin I got that belonged to ma granny. I belted oot the shop sharp at six and got the bus hame. I headed straight fur the bathroom, yelling to ma mammy that I didnae have time fur any tea but to tell ye the truth, I couldnae have eaten a bite. I washed the smell of veg and bashed fruit off me and then I pit on ma best skirt and jumper and startit on ma hair. It's that straight that it never stays put but I backcombed it like mad and then tried to gie it a wee flick oot at the sides like yon singer. I made masel up wi pancake and lipstick and some of mammy's eau de cologne. I suppose I looked aw right but I knew I wisnae as good as mammy claimed.

'My, yer that bonny,' she kept saying. 'And that grown-up looking. Yer no ma wee lassie any mair.'

And on and on she went while I was silently wishing she'd stop it. I felt I was on ma way to ma execution rather than ma first dance. And all because I wantit a keek at Pauline's lumber. I suppose I could have said I didnae feel like going but by the time I'd explained it all to ma mammy and faced up to Pauline and Sheena on the Monday, I decided I'd best get it over with. Sheena's got a tongue on her that kin spit oot venom and I didnae want to end up being the class isolate like Soapy Bubble if she decided to have a go at me fur backing oot at the last minute.

I teetered doon to the bus stop in ma stilettos. I was early as I jist wantit oot the hoose as soon as I could so I stood there freezing till Pauline and Sheena came.

'Have we missed the 37?' Pauline asked. We were jist aboot blue before the bus arrived and we climbed upstairs. The conductor came rushing up for wur fares and Sheena brought oot her Benson and Hedges as well.

'Sumday's in the money,' Pauline said.

'Got the money aff ma dad,' said Sheena. 'He thinks I'm gaun to spend it on a book fur English. D'ye want one?'

She passed the packet to Pauline and then to me.

'Thanks, naw,' I said, 'they Benson's bowfin. I prefer Passing Cloud.' I wisnae gonnae let on that the only time I'd had a fag was when playing Monopoly with ma ither pals and we'd sooked on wan between us till the end was aw drookit and we was coughing like mad.

The bus journey didnae take long enough fur me and I clambered aff the bus behind the two of them and we crossed the road and walked up the path to the scout hall. It was aw lit up and there were quite a few folk queuing.

'Aw fur gawd's sake,' Sheena said to Pauline, 'I tellt ye to get a move on. See if we didnae get in, I'll be that scunnered.'

Pauline was too busy eyeing up everybody to see if she could spot her lumber frae the week afore to be bothered. I couldnae have cared less if we didnae get in or no. In fact I was secretly wishing we were too late and the place was already packed but no, we were paying ower the money and heading fur the cloakroom afore I knew it.

I could have stayed there aw night but Pauline was dead keen to look fur her lumber, James, his name was. So I had to follow them oot into the hall where the band was playing trad jazz. It soundit great and I felt ma feet wanting to tap as I like dancin and I'm no bad at it. Sheena got ta'en up almost right away and Pauline was eyeing aw the guys looking fur her James. It was getting that crowded with folk pushing their way in and we were aw crushed up at the back and mair and mair folk were ga'en on to the dance flair.

Pauline gi'ed me a nudge and I could tell from the look on her face that she'd seen James. She pointed him oot to me. He wisnae that much to look at, nothing like the Adonis she'd made him oot to be. She played the 'whit a surprise to see ye here' game and the pair of them headed on to the flair. I was left staunin masel like a big stooky so after a few minutes I stertit to wonder whit to dae next. The music stopped and the flair cleared a bit but neither Pauline or Sheena came back. Pauline was obviously still with James and Sheena must have got a lumber.

I shoved ma way through the crowd so's it wid look like I'd jist cam off the dance flair and moved to anither part of the hall. The music stertit up again and again I was left staunin on ma ain. I stood there tapping ma feet and trying to look like I was fair enjoying masel when I felt sumdy pushing me towards the flair. I was that chuffed because the band were playing ma favourite tune Wimoweh and I had a right big grin on ma face when I turned roon and saw it was Soapy Bubble. Aw naw, I thought. Anybody but him. I couldnae say no now that I was on the flair, so I jist had to dance with him. He danced like wan of they string puppet things, feet gaun aw ways and no in time. I could see Pauline hinging on to James and jigging aboot in perfect rhythm but I couldnae see Sheena. I wisnae sure whether or no I was happy to be dancin, anybody but Soapy Bubble would've been great, but at least I wisnae a wallflower any mair.

I was jist beginning to relax a bit when I seen James and Pauline sniggering and looking at us. Soapy Bubble didnae see them and danced us right ower in front of them. Jist as we joogled by, James spat at us and the spittle landed on the back of Soapy's jaikit. James was laughing and wan or two of the couples beside us saw the stuff sliding doon Soapy's back and stertit laughing too. I felt something in me kinda explode. Okay, Soapy was a bit of an eejit but who did that ponce James think he was, daen a thing like that? He may have been posh but he didnae act it. And as fur ma supposit friend Pauline, I'd seen her fur whit she was and I didnae like it.

We was still dancin aboot and I was that angry with James that I steered Soapy towards him and Pauline and pushed his back against her. The spittle rubbed on to her haun and I could see her face when she looked doon and realised whit the wet stuff was. She stopped dancin and stood there trying to tell James whit it was and asking fur a hankie aff him. When he realised it was his own slavers on her haun, he glowered at me. I pretended I hadnae seen and it was nothing to dae with us and I scooted Soapy across the flair well away from them. As soon as the music stopped I was away aff the flair, no even waiting fur Soapy to lead me back. I ran intae the cloakroom again and jist got ma coat and left wi'oot saying anything to Pauline or Sheena. I couldnae go straight home or ma mammy wid ken I was home early so I walked fur miles back to ma ain part of the toon. I was frozen and ma feet were killing me but I tellt ma mammy I'd been dancin that much I'd near ta'en ma toes aff and that we'd hud to wait ages fur a bus.

'Ye wurny staunin winchin at the bus stop and no noticing the buses, were ye?' and I could tell she was back in the past again.

'Naw,' I said but I hung ma heid and she thought I was lying but I didnae care, so long as it made her happy.

I went straight aff to bed and turned on Radio Luxemburg deid loud so's she widnae hear me sobbing under the bedclaes. I knew whit I wid face on the Monday.

Comma

JIM HUGHES

Did you notice me?
In that beautiful line,
that heart stopping phrase?

Did you notice me?
I bet you didn't.

Just a comma, the lowest ranking foot soldier
in punctuation's pecking order.

Smaller than a colon, the dictionary defines me.
A colon: two specks of fly shit on the page
of history.

But me, this tail of mine relates me to my
glamorous cousin.
That flaming longhaired star, the comet.

So when next you hold your breath,
in that blissful hiatus that heightens desire,
think of me.

That pause
comma
between this heartbeat
comma
and the next.

The Cry

Kate Ayres

I was stillborn in the front bedroom of my grandmother's house on the town hill, overlooking Swansea Bay, where the lights of the town meet the black of the sea.

The doctor, who had arrived late, in his pyjamas and drunk as a lord, solemnly, soberly informed my father that, sadly, his firstborn's time of birth and death would be one and the same.

My father looked at the flushed, expectant, excited face of my mother at the head of the bed and then at my grandmother, pale and shrunk with shock, shaking her head at the foot of the bed. He knew his five brothers-in-law and one sister-in-law were on the stairs, holding hands and breath, waiting to hear a baby cry.

He wondered how he would get through the next ten awful minutes, the next hour, day, week, life.

He thought about the white wooden cot and the flagship navy blue pram, the tiny white knitted, neatly, expectantly folded clothes in the new bought-on-credit chest of drawers in 'the baby's room' at home. He thought about being a father, pushing a pram and a swing and a beaming, toothless smile below oddly familiar eyes. He thought about his own father and how he had thought he would be a better father.

He thought about how he had longed to meet the foot that had kicked him at night through the confinement of skin and womb. He thought about telling his wife that despite the last eight months and especially the last eight hours, that she was not a mother. He thought about telling his mother that she was not a grandmother.

He looked into the vast black space where the lights of the town become the sea and he started to cry.

The midwife, who had also delivered my mother and had delayed her retirement to see me safely into the world, turned to my grandmother.

'I'll not lose this one,' she said.

The whisky weary physician, embarrassed by his helplessness and the sight of another man crying wished he had taken the time to put on his suit. He was deafened by the ear drum splitting silent disappointment in him and wondered how soon he could leave. He was put in his place by the midwife who had seen his type and worse more times than she cared to remember.

'You look after the mother, I'll see to the child.'

The sister was sent for hot and cold water, one of the brothers to a neighbour for brandy, as my grandfather had signed the pledge and would not have the drink in the house.

I was cold and blue and flat, I imagine that I may have been floating down a tunnel toward a bright light, but I couldn't tell you for sure.

My body was dunked, biscuit fashion, from hot to cold to cold to hot until my fragile heart had no choice but to beat in shock and my innocent soul was snatched back from the gates of heaven, which is surely where never-lived babies go.

Flushed and worried, my uncle, who was now, however briefly, an uncle arrived with the next but one's Christmas liquor. The first taste of life in my mouth was not from my mother's breast but from a tarnished Sheffield steel teaspoon. I like to think, that in the chaos, a silver spoon could not be found.

Then, nappied and swaddled, I was placed in the waiting crib with an old fashioned earthenware bottle. The doctor, lately sober, and the family, wanting a drink, left.

My mother, still high on gas and air and the birth experience, was giddy and oblivious to the gentle sympathy, the white-faced, shocked anticipation of the sorrow to come. My grandmother, who had birthed enough still, silent babies of her own, was, in her indomitable style, already mentally cooking the ham for the funeral tea. My father trying to move his lips around the unsaid words needing to be said, dry tears on his cheeks.

After a time, my mother slipped into sleep, exhausted by her transition into motherhood. The midwife crossed the space between the crib and the bed and touched my sleeping mother's empty arm.

'I'll not lose this one.' With a straight look at my father and a promise to return in four hours, she left also.

My father lay down next to my mother, sensually aware of the space that I had left in his wife's belly, now taking up space in the crib next to a hard brown china bottle. He lay stiffly awake and aware of the lack of movement or sound from the crib.

After three hours he slid from the blankets and avoided the crib on his way to the kitchen where he brewed and smoked and met his nervous, unhopefully expectant in-laws.

My grandmother asked if I had cried. Not a peep, was his response and the implication of the words hung over the tea cups and the smoking ashtray with a finality that was uncomfortably understood.

Altogether close mouthed, full of unknown knowledge, wanting but not wanting to speak, so full of unspoken sympathy and compassion but not wanting to say, not wanting to be the first to say. To a husband and father who didn't want to hear the words they were going to have to say, so they brewed and smoked and waited.

A sharp tap at the door announced the arrival of the midwife, pale and unslept also.

'Has she cried?'

The shocked faces around the table shook as one.

'It's probably best if I take her now, I'll do what has to be done. You'll need to register her, Births and Deaths.' To my father who felt old and spent.

With sore throats and gritty eyes they brewed and drank some more. With unwilling legs they climbed the stairs to the front bedroom of the house on the town hill overlooking the sea.

My mother breathed easy, slept the sweet sleep of the unknowing in the bed where she had become a mother and would soon be told that she was no longer a mother. Her mother stood at the foot of the bed, worrying what she would say to her daughter about her daughter.

My father looked at the flickering lights of Swansea town from the front bedroom of my grandmother's house on the town hill overlooking Swansea Bay and at the darkness where the town becomes the sea.

The midwife crept up on the crib and took the warming bottle, now cold and useless and placed it gently on the floor next to the redundant crib.

She thought of all the babies she had brought safely into this world, but this one, her last, the one she would remember, more than all the others, but for the wrong reason. She lifted me from the cold crib and brought my face up to hers. I opened my eyes and my mouth and I started to cry.

Twenty four years later, supported by her sticks and grateful, respectful hands, the midwife, my midwife, my mother's midwife, stood at my wedding and told this story.

We all cried.

A Bonnie Fechter

Sheila Templeton

That winter, snaw flew its feathers thick
smoorichin the hale Rannoch Moor.
I thocht the warld wud be white for iver.
Danny the Keeper said the stags
wud have tae come doon,
else they'd sterve tae death.

We'd niver seen red deer afore.
But these beasts wernae ony shade o red.
Ivery day as the licht hid ahint the Black Mounth,
they floated ower the high fence
at the side o the line,
sepia angels biggen a brig ower cloudy drifts
against a grape slate sky. I thocht their hooves
could niver touch the grun,

until the day we heard a scraping
ootside the kitchen door. He was big.
His antlers telt a lang story, a hero's story,
of territory defended and hinds protected.
He eased back a bittie, but didnae flee.
At my mither's nod, I threw the tattie peelings
scudding intae the kirned up khaki snaw.

And waited and watched while he took his time,
his fine big heid lowered wi nae loss o dignity.
And so he lat me feed him ivery day,
as the licht left the sky.
Nae to touch or stroke, but he'd lat me
look intae his een and watch him,

until the day he didnae come. The day I looked
and shouted and poked aboot the frosty dyke.
But nae use. My pail o slippy tattie parings frozen
in the night where I'd left it.
I splashed bilin water tae saften it for him.
But nae sign.

Winter gnawed on,

until Danny the Keeper said ower a nip and a fag
'Thon's a grand auld beast
deid doon by the burn.
Funny that. How they hide awa,
when they ken it's their time.
Like an auld war hero.
Like ony bonnie fechter
fan he kens his time is up.'

Keeping Promises

JANICE JOHNSTON

But I promised, you see. Cross my heart and hope to die. I can't break a promise.

He didn't make me promise.

I screamed and screamed till my throat was sore, but he kept on hurting me. Then I begged and begged him to stop, but he didn't listen. It was only when I promised, cross my heart and hope to die, that he stopped. Then he looked right at my face for the first time.

'I promise I won't tell. Cross my heart and hope to die,' I whispered, looking into his eyes. I tried not to breathe his breath.

He laughed then stood up, brushing leaves and dead grass from his jumper. He stared at me, crossed his heart with his finger, slowly, and then left. So I had to keep my promise, see?

I knew who he was. The big boys called him Pedo. One time, some people threw dog dirt at his windows. Another time, some people painted rude words on his walls. Then the police talked to Chelsea Scott's big brothers and it all stopped.

Afterwards, when he saw me in the street, or in the Co-op, he crossed his heart with his finger, slowly, and I knew he remembered my promise.

It was my fault.

All our mums tell us not to cut across the back lane on our

own. We never listen. If we go the long way round it takes forever. That day I was supposed to meet Chelsea but mum sent me for milk. By the time I got to the swings, Chelsea had gone.

I was pretty sure she'd go to the multi-storey. She likes to be where the big girls are. I might have gone home in a huff but I'd made her a new scoubee – blue and green – and I wanted to see if she liked it. I'd spent ages getting each bit straight and the twists were the best. All the other girls had pink and white and orange scoubees and the boys all wanted them in their football team's colours. No one else would have a blue and green one except Chelsea. Chelsea always wants to be different.

I could hear mum's voice in my head telling me not to cut across the back lane on my own but I wanted to find Chelsea quickly.

It wasn't till I passed the slide and the roundabout and ducked down under the overhanging branches that I remembered it was Friday and the factory closed early on Fridays. There would be no one shouting, no thumping machinery, and no forklift zooming about.

When I heard rustling in the bushes I began to run. Then I tripped and his hand came out of the bushes and grabbed me.

Then I promised, cross my heart and hope to die, and he stopped and went away.

And I went home. I told mum I fell and she yelled at me for tearing my new top but when I started to cry – great, deep sobs that frightened both of us – she hugged me tight. She tried to get me to tell her what was wrong but I couldn't say, could I?

I had to make a new scoubee for Chelsea; I couldn't find the first one. I made her new one, purple and yellow. It wasn't as good as the first one but Chelsea still liked it.

I thought I'd dropped the first scoubee but when I saw him – Pedo – in the Co-op I knew I hadn't. I didn't want to look into his eyes again so I stared at his hands. That was nearly as bad. I could remember his long fingers twisting round my arms and pinning me to the ground. He was jingling his keys in his hand. Then I saw he had the blue and green scoubee fastened on to his key ring. He saw me staring and twisted it between his fingers then crossed his heart with one finger, slowly.

I forgot about the bread I was supposed to be buying and ran home. Mum yelled at me again but I didn't care.

So now I'm waiting at the swings for Chelsea again. I've been waiting for ages and she's really late but she made me promise to wait for her, cross my heart and hope to die, and she knows I always keep my promises.

He – Pedo – passed by a little while ago. I watched him hurry up from the back lane. He came past the roundabout and the slide and walked right by the swings.

He did the crossing his heart thing again and I watched the blue and green scoubee swinging on his key ring. He had another scoubee dangling there – a purple and yellow one.

But I promised, you see. Cross my heart and hope to die.

Portrait of a Lady

NORMAN BISSETT

We caught the Number Five from Marco Polo
To Piazzale Roma, for the water bus.
Bellini, Tintoretto, Tiepolo
Slumbered nearby. The cold affected us,
A raw, low-season haar rising like ague
from the swamp to clutch our throats.
As if in bird-beaked masks against the plague,
Some shivering locals, shrouded in fur coats
And sooty capes, tricorned and sinister,
sat sullen as the tomb. Lost in the dark,
we drifted by each creaking, shadowy pier
till at San Zaccaria, we disembarked,
with Calle della Rasse still to come –
through which we found our home away from home.

Snow fell like feathers into the lagoon.
The bell-tower stood accused of cowardice.
We watched the obliteration of the moon
as side-canals slowly filled up with ice.
A white-out blizzarded across the square,
veiling from the view the horses and domes.
The streets fell silent. There was no one there
and all the gondolieri stayed at home.
We looked outside to witness at first light
this shining pearl, the Adriatic queen,
resplendent and unsullied, virgin-white,
La Serenissima grown ever more serene –
the old seductress putting on a show
and rising like a phoenix from the snow.

Drinking Jesus' Blood

MICHAEL MALONE

Sister Mary tears me from my dream,
mouth pursed white like the lip of a drawstring bag.
Again, urine had seeped from my Judas bladder.
Pyjamas in deep, wet, cotton folds burn from belly to knee.

Sister Mary, a window-less room and a bath of ice water.
The drum in my ear shivers
at the machine gun rattle of my teeth.
Naked, I hide my hairless sex behind bone-thin hands.
'Get your hands away, you dirty little pervert.'
My mouth opens, my hands move from sin, then back.

Cold water bites flesh.
Skin and muscle shrink to a tight sheath.
Her black sleeves rolled up,
forearms white as a frosted soul.
She tries to find suds in iced carbolic.
I bite on the questions:
will my teeth chip or break from clattering,
how much will the tooth fairy give if they are in crumbs?
Rubbed with stiff towel till skin heats, blue to pink.

In the Sacristy with Jim Docherty, the other Altar Boy,
itch of shame replaces the nip of urine.
'Wet The Bed,' he chants.
'Shut it, Big Nose,' I bruise his arm – and don white.
'Lads,' says Father Kieran, tousles our brylcreemed heads
and leaves us with a chalice full of communion wine.

The vessel grows until it shrinks the room,
I lean forward to touch it.
Jim's eyebrows bounce off his hairline, 'Bet you wouldn't.'
I grip the stem in answer to his hushed taunt.
Heart charging at my ribcage I moisten lips, and pour.
Teeth and tongue fur sour before I force open my throat.
A blazing bolus flares a trail to my stomach.

Jim, slack mouthed with fear and awe,
'Oh-oh, that's a sin. You've just drank Jesus' blood.'
'Aye, and it tastes like piss!'

He Ain't Heavy

DES DILLON

It's an old Victorian sandstone bridge with the BBC at one end and posh houses at the other. It must've looked good in its heyday but now it's lined with cars so you never see its full splendour.

But I was walking slow that day. I had time to spare and summer was coming in. A young woman brushed past as if the world was an unnecessary impediment. Even her curves and the glossy backs of her thighs were hateful. Halfway across was sat this guy. He started singing at her.

♫You're gorgeous, I'd do anything for you.

She tracks a safe trail between him and the dusty line of parked cars. But his song followed telling her how gorgeous she was. The further she got the more his singing distorted to shouting. He stopped singing when she turned the corner but kept watching as if she might come back.

I gave him a fright when I said,

—Looks like she's not coming back.

He looked up and into my eyes before he spoke.

—They never come back, he said and took a slug of warm cider from a blue plastic bottle. And the way he said they never come back had a sort of weight in it. A something that made me think.

—She's BBC, he said when he'd drained the bottle. And that explained it. He had a couple of recent cuts on his baldy head and his right fist was scabbed up.

—Fall out with a door?

—Brick wall he said, bang! And he mimed punching a wall.

—Used to do that all the time, I said, showing him the scars on my knuckles. He checked them and believed with a nod.

—I'm always fuckin doing that me, he said.

—You from Blackpool?

He was from Burnley. His eyes were blue. His clothes had been clean a couple of days ago. But even though it was getting hot, he didn't smell except for cider and nicotine. I told him how I used to live in Blackpool but he didn't want to know. He wanted to get the subject well out of Lancashire. Told me how he flits from Ireland to Scotland. Cork in the winter, Inverness in summer.

—See this, this here bridge, it's a top of the pops spot this is. People going by all the time, okay toffs they are, but sometimes they drop me the brass like eh? And d'you know what the good bit is?

I didn't.

—I can see up their skirts.

I was still laughing when he said no that's not what it was.

—Cops cannot see me when they drive past. All cops can see is line of cars and bobbing heads of beautiful people on their way to the BBC. That's how I got the cuts on head and the busted fist me. Cops came up in George Square asked me to move on. Gave them a barrow load of fucks so they arrested me. I struggled and in drunken rage I laid into bottom of big statue.

—Aye, I said, —I'm like a Gremlin on the drink an all.

He burst out laughing. —Gremlin. Fuckin Gremlin, that's a good one, he said, —Fancy going for a sup?

—No. Can't. Been off it fifteen years, I said.

He looked at me. Held my gaze in those powerful blue eyes and said, —Congratulations on your fifteenth birthday.

Well, him saying that: he knew what it meant and I knew what it meant. And he held his hand out and we shook. As he tightened his grip he cried. His grip got so tight I thought he was going to fall right through that bridge into the river fifty feet below.

Then he started singing.

♫Happy birthday to you…

And he laughed.

And I laughed.

And he sang.

♫Happy birthday to you…

And some posh folks went by but he sung as if I was the only person in the world. He wasn't being caustic. He was genuine. I stood there and took it. Like I deserved it. And looking at him I realised I deserved something. Whatever had happened, luck or chance or Divine Intervention – it wasn't me on that bridge it was him. And the twists and turns that brought us here would be miniscule. Little decisions that led to little actions that gathered together to form a path. This was the day two paths crossed. And we spoke about that. In those terms. We didn't shirk from the spirituality of width or the philosophy of depth. We mined that subject till we'd dug up truth. And by the end of it we were joined somewhere.

Then I told him about David. My brother. Who's down and out an all. In another town. I told him a funny story about the day I went up a close and there he was, my brother with three other alkies. About how he gave me a hard time. And how hard it was for me with all the guilt and self-loathing cos I wanted out of there, away from my brother.

—But you stayed.

—Aye I stayed, but I wanted out of there.

—But you stayed, he said, —You fuckin well stayed.

—He's my brother, I said.

He caught my eye and said this:

—That's right. He is your brother.

And he thumped his chest three times lightly. There was something holy about they way he done it. If people were passing I don't know. But I'll tell you this; there was something happened in that moment. My heart sprung open and compassion flowed freely out. Or the impediments to my compassion broke away. Or the world's compassion flowed in. Or something. Some

thing

He seen it and he winked.

—Aye he said, and winked, —I'm the same. But I just can't break free.

—Listen, I said reaching out to shake his hand, —Thanks.

—You know what I'm going to say now don't you?

I didn't. But it felt like it would be profound.

—Few quid for a charge?

I gave him a fiver and he thanked me with a wink and a punch on the arse as I walked away. I was nearly at the other end of the bridge when he shouted.

—Hey!

I turned. He stretched his arms up and sang. His Opera singer voice had everybody looking.

♫He ain't heavy, he sang, —He's my Brother. His welfare is my concern. So on we go.

I laughed, gave him a fist in the air and turned the corner. At first I thought he was talking about David. But then I realised exactly what he meant.

Andrew

Marion Montgomery

Why me? You Scots shuid hae a sodger saint
Like George the dragon-slayer.
Or if ye maun choose frae the Twelve
Tak James or John, the sons of thunder, fierce
Agin auld neebor foe, Samaria,
Or zealot Simon wantin shot o Rome.
Thomas wi his doubts, or speirin Philip
Wid suit ye better nor a fisher lad
Wha didnae argue or ding sinners doon,
Jist listened and ca'd ither fowk tae hear.

But some chiel brocht ma banes tae this grey shore.
Its kirk in ruins, and its harbour silted,
Whaur can I cast my net for fish or men?
Syne I maun staun for Scotland,
Please God she too will share her loaves
And fishes wi the lave and keep an open mind.

Song of Wallace

Rowena M Love

'I have brought you to the ring, now see if you can dance[1]*'*

In the discord of distant days,
seven hundred years ago,
came this hero
on a legendary scale,
his huge sword a baton
conducting men in pitched battle
until betrayal's false note spoiled the tune.
To the enemy's chorus of jeers,
the Guardian faced his grisly death
with the same pride and courage
he'd led his life –
and ours.

Dead but not silenced,
for Wallace was more than a passing note
in the libretto of liberty
sung by so many Scots –
his was the very melody at its core;
a leitmotiv of patriotism
guaranteed,
even now,
to stir the blood
at the merest echo of his name
and have our hearts dancing.

[1] Wallace's words to his army before the battle of Falkirk

The Towering Wallace

Marion Reid

I'm standing here, looking up,
Heeled at the Wallace Tower,
A totem on High Street, Ayr.
Traffic is swirling around me –
Tourists, buses and shoppers.

Miles to the north, long ago,
A freedom fighter was born,
Young William vowed to restore
Scotland to national glory.
His story of life remains misty…

But do not be mistaken. His end
Was a definite document –
Sly shifting of side – Betrayal!
A brutal hanging in London,
A life given bravely for country.

A Knight with an army of sorts,
He fought a cat-and-mouse battle,
In Ayrshire, on its dip and slope,
Across Scotland, for its liberty.
His cause, alone, never wavered.

His good strong arm with its sword
Rises above us, high on the Tower,
A presence still felt. Local hero.
Crowds follow on, walk beneath
The stature of tall William Wallace.

Tongue-Tied

FIONA ATCHISON

He squinted at the computer screen in order to get a better look and wondered if he dare enter the online chat room. Suddenly the front door slammed shut and a female voice called to him from the hallway. If she found him using the computer again at this time of day, she would start to get suspicious. As quickly and silently as possible he closed the screen down. Her head swung round the door 'Okay dear? Sorry I'm late. I'll just put the tea on – got your favourite.'

His mind quickly conjured up the image of two small plastic bags, each containing a part of a human tongue. And at this present time, they were languishing in the freezer.

He nodded with a smile and gave her the thumbs up.

DCI Joyce Stokes showered quickly, cursing the fact she would be late on her first day back at the station. The honeymoon in Paris had been wonderful, but now it was back to rainy Glasgow. She caught the tail end of Trevor Parker's comment as she walked to her desk, '…looking a bit the worse for wear, eh boys?'

As Joyce drew Trevor a contemptuous glare she was aware of the stout figure of DI Tom Baxter standing in front of the crime board, eager to get started.

'Okay everyone let's have some shush can we? Last night a

young man, now identified as Joss White, was found dead in an alleyway off Renfield Street. As you can see from the photographs, the cause of death appears to be from the number of stab wounds to his back and,' Baxter paused, 'there's something else – half his tongue was missing. That's the *same* MO as Jim Mackay four weeks ago, who was found on the floor of his tenement close in Easterhouse. He'd suffered multiple stab wounds to his back, and his tongue had been partially removed. Same cause of death, which means, lads and lassies – get me some answers before the press have a field day.'

'So, are you saying it could be the same killer, boss? A serial killer like?' Trevor asked.

'Let's look for some evidence first shall we? It may be a possibility or perhaps it's a copycat kill from the papers' cover of the first murder.' Tom glared around the room. 'Just let's pray this corpse's leads don't go as cold as the last.'

He felt a release of tension today. She had decided to visit her mum in Paisley and he could use the time to plan. He peered out the living room window through a gap in the blind. The car was gone. He double-checked; yes the front door was locked. Back in his bedroom his heart thumped hard as he entered an online chat room. He started to type:

'You don't know why Mackay and White are dead, but I do. This is a warning, to the police – leave well alone and no one else will get hurt.'

His rucksack was packed and all he needed now was to get the front door key and leave.

When Joyce got back home around 7.30 pm she found husband Chris in the kitchen reading the paper. 'Hi love,' he said reaching for her. This was the part of the day she liked best, curling up on the settee with Chris, a glass of red wine, and the aroma of a pre-timed casserole wafting from the oven. She settled down and began to rethink her findings of the day.

There had been a breakthrough. It was now two days following the murder of Joss White. Joyce had interviewed several of his social work colleagues trying to source any similarities or contact, between White and Mackay. She grimaced, the murders were now known locally as the 'double dram murders' because of a popular blend of whisky labelled 'White & Mackay'.

White was a student social worker in his final year on placement with Glasgow City Council. His Supervisor, Rae Brown, and colleagues were shocked at his death. The six cases he'd been working on were currently being scrutinised by the police, but it was proving hard to find any probable connection to Mackay.

They knew Jim Mackay was 28, single and a loner, who'd had various jobs. None seemed to last longer than a year or so. He'd some previous form stealing and driving cars as a teenager. His latest stint was with the Volunteer Drivers' Association (VDA), working for mileage rates. So far it didn't look as if the victims' paths had met, but the possibility factor niggled at Joyce. The list of Mackay's pick-ups for the previous three months had been investigated and found to consist of school runs to Special Schools. Despite hard police work, there were no leads.

'Are you sure Joss has not had some contact with the VDA, through another colleague perhaps?' Joyce persisted, questioning his supervisor again.

Rae rubbed her eyes tiredly for a moment or two, then suddenly perked up. 'Wait a minute, staff have to take a turn at 'duty', which means technically Joss could receive calls from anyone.' She walked over to a desk and slowly began to turn the pages of an A4 book. Rae's voice was almost a whisper as she looked up at Joyce in alarm. Her finger pointed to a line in the book. 'Oh God! He did make a call to the Volunteer Drivers' Centre. According to this entry about a month ago, 3rd of September.'

'Can you tell who the transport was ordered for and at what time?' Joyce's voice was quick and sharp with anticipation. She knew the date of the request to be only two days before Jim Mackay was found murdered.

Rae punched out a reference number from the log into her computer, and a name appeared – 'Daniel Hart'. Tapping a few more keys, a file of case notes appeared on the screen. Rae scrolled down. 'Joss arranged transport for this 21 year old man, who apparently required to attend a hospital appointment last month. He's a wheelchair user. Previous road traffic accident, three years ago according to this.'

It had been a shock that the volunteer driver, Jim, had recognised him. He had no recollection of the actual accident at all, just waking up in hospital without being able to feel his legs. But worst of all, finding he could no longer talk, or more importantly, no longer sing. He could only vaguely remember his past life. A life when he was eighteen years old, able-bodied and on his way to the airport early one morning to catch a flight. He'd been accepted to study at The London School of Music. That very day instead of his life just beginning, it had sickeningly ended.

DCI Trevor Parker was bursting with news for Joyce and the DI. He'd questioned the VDA driving co-ordinator again who remembered the regular afternoon driver for 3rd September had failed to turn in. Mackay just happened to be in the office at the time. White had phoned in on spec and asked for a driver at short notice. Daniel Harts's mother had made the request. Apparently she hadn't felt well enough to drive him to the hospital herself as she usually did.

'The absentee driver's name was still entered in their book for that afternoon,' Parker explained. 'But it was our victim, Mackay who actually did the run. The entry was never corrected.'

Baxter's small frame sprang into action. 'Right, get over quickly to Daniel Hart's address. This new information links White and Mackay – a lead we missed first time round.'

It had been a surreal conversation, Daniel recalled, and one sided. Jim Mackay, the guy sent round from the Volunteer Drivers' Centre had recognised him straight away. He'd actually confessed to being the other driver involved in his accident! Mackay told Daniel he'd felt really guilty and followed events in the newspaper. He'd explained to him how upset he'd been on learning that Daniel was so badly injured. Sitting, unable to speak, Daniel felt a fury rise in him that he found hard to control.

Joyce and Trevor walked up the wheelchair ramp leading to Daniel Hart's front door. Trevor rapped the knocker smartly and winked at Joyce, 'Hope he doesn't try to make a run for it.'

'I see you passed your disability awareness training then.'

The door slowly opened revealing a tall, wiry woman who smiled as they explained who they were. 'Daniel's in his room at the moment, I think he may be sleeping, he gets very tired by teatime,' she explained. 'I'm his mother, so if I can be of any help?'

Joyce sat down on the offered chair. There was a smell of stale alcohol hanging around the room. 'Mrs Hart, we believe you ordered a Volunteer Driver for your son through social services, about a month ago or so to take him to hospital?' she enquired.

'Yes that's right, I had a migraine. I get them from time to time and can't drive. Affects my vision you see. Why are you asking?'

'The man who drove your son that day Mrs Hart, was called Jim Mackay,' Joyce replied.

'He was murdered two days later,' Trevor interrupted abruptly. 'The person you made the driving request to, Joss White, was also found dead, earlier this week.'

Mrs Hart reached for a glass and took a small sip. 'That's dreadful, those poor young men…but what's this got to do with Daniel?'

Joyce spoke softly. 'Mrs Hart, does your son sometimes go out in the evenings – on his own?'

He could hear his mother's voice and that of two other people talking in the next room but couldn't make out what they were saying. He had a good idea it was the police though. She'd told him to pretend he was asleep, so he'd transferred himself from his wheelchair to bed. What was she going to say?

Tom Baxter, DI, sat opposite Joyce in the canteen. After a short debrief involving the visit to Daniel Hart, everyone seemed a bit deflated. The only lead they had was of a young disabled man, whom they would return to try to question the next day. Apparently, he never went out of the house unaccompanied. Apart from needing to use a wheelchair, he had no speech and poor vision. Not top of the list as suspect material. Mrs Hart had given her son a cast iron alibi for the evenings in question. They were home together every night usually watching television.

On the road to the hospital Jim had started talking and it seemed he couldn't stop.

'The car came flying round a blind corner. I didn't have time to think never mind try to avoid you. I was lucky, a few cuts but it's a wonder we weren't all killed.'

Daniel, unable to speak, had sat in shock trying to take in what he was hearing. What did Mackay mean by 'all'? In the weeks following the accident he knew that he'd been found alone in the car, a victim, supposedly of a hit and run. Had there been a passenger in Mackay's car? He wished he'd taken his 'talk-type-writer' with him to ask.

Next morning a call came into the station from the Police IT section. Baxter relayed the news. 'You're not going to believe this, but a warning note regarding the killings of White and Mackay has been posted in a chat-room website and traced to Daniel Hart's computer.'

'A hundred percent sure boss?' Trevor asked.

'Well, a hundred percent his computer, but maybe he's not the only one with access remember,' Joyce added. She could have kicked herself for not insisting on questioning Daniel the evening before.

Five minutes later, Joyce and Trevor stood knocking at the front door of Daniel Hart's house, gaining no reply.

'Let's try round the back,' said Trevor.

Mackay had kept talking. 'It was the woman driving your car who told me to sling my hook. She warned me she'd pin the blame on me if I said anything to the polis or anyone. And I'm sorry pal, but I didn't need telling twice. What I could never fathom was, how come you were found alone and in the driving seat? Where did she disappear to?'

A penny suddenly clanged in Daniel's head. The vivid flashback memories he'd had after the accident were not figments of his imagination. In these dreams he could visualise his mother insisting on driving that morning. He'd tried to stop her – she'd been drinking as usual. In the end he'd thought it wasn't worth the hassle, because he would soon be away from her.

Daniel felt his blood chill. His own mother had caused the accident, and then hauled him into the driver's seat and left him to his injuries.

Steps led up to a glass paned door. Through it they could see the figure of a young man slumped in his wheelchair. Trevor broke a pane of glass and put his hand inside to unlock the door.

Jim Mackay had returned Daniel home after his hospital appointment. She'd come to the door, staggering slightly as she always did during a binge. But he'd caught the look on her face as she'd stared into the eyes of Mackay. Neither said a word, but that glimpse of mutual recognition had been enough.

She'd tried to act as if everything was normal. But when he'd heard about the murder of Jim Mackay, then poor Joss White, he knew…

Entering the kitchen, Joyce nearly fell over the prone body of Mrs Hart, lying in a pool of congealed blood. On searching the house, forensics made the grisly discovery of two severed tongues, now undergoing DNA testing. The young disabled man was being questioned at the station. He had an advocate with him and answered questions using a talk-type-writer. As his story unfolded, Joyce listened incredulously. A bitter, alcoholic woman had almost killed her son, and then murdered two innocent young men three years later thinking she was keeping her awful secret from him. Mackay had been killed because he had recognised her. Joss White's only crime had been to order a volunteer driver for her son. She couldn't take the risk, but ironically killing White had led the police straight to her. They could only guess why she had severed her victims' tongues – a symbol perhaps of their silence.

His mother had started drinking heavily when the police left. He'd quietly transferred back into his wheelchair. She was drinking at the kitchen table, and tried to smile at him. 'Everything's okay now love,' she slurred. 'Mother's sorted it all out again.'

He typed 'Why did you leave me in the car?'

She stared at him for a long, long moment then shrugged her shoulders. 'I just panicked.'

He made a crying sound at the back of his throat. 'You ruined my life.'

She stood up unsteadily and hissed, 'And what about my life, what about me? You didn't think twice about leaving me alone to go to some fancy music school.' Her voice became bitter. 'You almost left me, just like your father. That will never happen again.'

His world became slow motion but his mind was clear as his hand reached to the cushion on his wheelchair, where he'd placed the kitchen knife.

Behind a Suburban Street

SYLVIA COHEN

Trees, dressed for autumn
Proud in a mass of colour
A flourish before death.

Through them,
Beyond an unseen brook
Houses half reveal themselves
A mosaic of bricks and glass
A patchwork of leaves and roofs.

A neighbour's willow weeps
Its song of sadness
Disdaining the riot of red berries
Golden shrubs and purple winter pansies,
Witnesses to life
In a dying season.

The morning sun
Throws its clear simple light on
Birds who nervously survey the lawn,
Watching for prey and predator alike,
Then startled, glide to safety
As a squirrel scampers,
Or a cat prowls.

And the sun, inevitably, tracks its journey
Across the autumn sky
Splashing its canvas with colours of fire
Throwing changing, unearthly light
Across the trees and gardens.

Sparrows, robins, birds for all seasons,
Ease themselves across the arc of heaven
Flying home to roost and rest
As owls get ready to hunt and cry.

In the dusk sky the trees darken
To shadow-plays, through which
The house lights shyly glint,
Reminding us of something long-ago –
The shivering pleasure of
Winding through dark, cold nights
To the warm-lit safety of home.

Obeahman

Maya Rae McLaughlin

He watched the long shaft of sunlight fall across the room like a Zulu's spear. The noise of the hut coming to life pulled his mind fully from the mystical embrace of slumber and lazily he swung his legs out of the bed.

He listened a while to the strident tones of his wife ordering her children around. 'Man caint git no peace,' he muttered to himself peevishly.

With the children dispatched to their various chores and his wife gone to clean other folk's houses, the place became silent once more. He sighed like a man sorely tried and dipped a wooden ladle into the calabash of fresh water his wife brought up from the stream every morning and drank deeply of its cool sweetness. Replacing the ladle he moved across to the battered stove to see if the coffeepot was still warm. Then he noticed it. Lying unobtrusively and half-hidden by the grubby gingham skirt the cooker wore. Tentatively he stretched out a hand before pulling it back and shuddering. He knew what it was. 'She hex me.'

He threw on his clothes and stepped out into the harsh brightness of the noontime veldt. At this time of day with all the able-bodied men in the fields, the women labouring at their endless jobs and the children either in the schoolhouse or helping their parents, the village was quiet with only the old ones and babies around. He ran fly, sullen, jet-black eyes along the row of huts allowing them to rest on the very last one which housed the Obeahman. He sent vicious darts of anger to both his wife and the shaman. 'Whyn't she speak to me? She coulda come to me first.'

Because he was used to lying to both others and himself, this statement did not seem in any way incongruous to him and he conveniently forgot all the times she had approached him, a problem with one of the children, lack of money – she was always complaining too. She was tired, she was ill, her eyes hurt, her back hurt. Lucky for her she had a man who was patient. Never once had he hit her – well not properly anyway. Leastways not the way you'd hit a man but she bruised easy although sometimes he'd swear she doctored them bruises right up so's they looked worse. And instead of hiding herself away until they faded, the woman was brazen, parading herself around the village with the marks he'd put on her freely on show. 'Shameless.' She was a good worker though, he'd give her that. But he wasn't so bad, not like she painted it. Didn't he always put food on the table whenever he won at cards and didn't he never, ever hit her unless she deserved it? 'Aint no reason fo' a hex.' She'd gone too far this time.

He went back inside and squatted down, studying the fetish lying there on the kitchen floor. It was wrapped up in a tight ball of grass and delicately laced with cobwebs. What was in there? A lock of his hair perhaps? He ran a hand across his skull looking for a bald spot where she could have shaved off his hair in the night. Or maybe some nail clippings?

He studied his hands and feet carefully. Hadn't she clipped his nails for him only a few nights before? He pushed his face as close as he dared but the bundle offered no clue and he could not risk empowering the hex further by laying his hands upon it. What if he ignored it? Would the hex disappear? 'A hex is a hex,' he decided and since the thing was hidden he wasn't expected to find it so from that he understood it didn't matter if he noticed it or not. A hex is a hex. His sly brain cartwheeled around in his head. He had to see the Obeahman and convince him to take the curse away. He took a deep breath and stepped into the sunlight.

'Hex caint never be taken 'way,' the shaman said 'but it can be returned to he who sent it.'

'Or she.'

'Or she,' the Obeahman agreed 'except I aint never put no hex on you and your wife never ask me to.'

'You lying!' He trembled, feeling a cold sweat prickle uncomfortably on his warm body.

'I don't need to lie,' the shaman said simply 'there is no hex, plain and simple.'

He left the hut with real fear now lodged in his belly. Was the Obeahman telling the truth? He offered money – more money than she could ever have paid – but still the man said no. He offered then his one good milking cow, his goat and half a year's profit from his wife's vegetable garden, but the Obeahman shook his head. In desperation he offered Msoto his eldest daughter fourteen now and ripe, but the Obeahman did not change his mind. 'Go home fool,' he'd said.

The fetish lay innocently on the floor and he wondered if it had the power to see him, to watch him and to know exactly when its power was going to kill him? He ran out of the hut and away from the village towards the town where he knew she'd be working. If he'd been thinking rationally he'd have known he never did listen to her chatterings long enough to know which house she'd be cleaning that day, but his mind was most irrational. Obeah gets you that way.

Unused to exertion, he was forced to slow his pace but the sweat still poured out of his body, from every orifice it flowed freely, his tongue was dry as dust and his heart hammered in his scrawny chest. Then his head began to spin, faster it went and pulsating too and he veered off the dirt track road into the wide-open veldt. His eyes saw yellow all around and his breathing came ragged and laboured. He lay face down in the coarse patchy scrub and a fierce stabbing pain made him clutch at his heart. He let his breath go slowly, trying to ease both panic and pain but the pain stabbed at him harder and the woolly yellow mist thickened before his eyes. Then the mist separated, became two distinctive shapes which loomed threateningly before him more hideous than he could ever imagine and he shut them out with his eyes.

Too late, he remembered the frail human eyelid is no match for Obeah mist and his fly, lazy eyes froze open in their final horror.

It was dusk by the time she got home. She sat down heavily on a stool in the small kitchen, her mind busy wondering what would fill their bellies tonight. She caught sight of something poking out from underneath the stove. She flicked a foot at it but it didn't move. Easing her tired bones downwards she squatted on the floor and pulled out a clump of dirty dried grass. 'Msoto,' she called 'you bin lettin' the goat git inside the house again?'

island man does a Dylan

KNOTBROOK TAYLOR

(upon hearing a Gaelic poet recite)

Words come in waves; line after rhythmic line
tide an irreversible glottology; swept by secret syllables
a headland battered; by pelagic phrase
alphabet of the machair; landscape; morphology
and the names; the names he names
seduce; inveigle
to be a grain; a petal; a downward tendril
a mind imbued with inheritance
a choppy sea; his choppy sea
his keen mourning for that morning when
we all speak homogenous; one tongue

you may rip open your shirt; you may lament
shape the phonics of Hebridean rain
tinkering on corrugated rust

(somewhere flood the falls; dark and unclear; your falls)
I envy those teeth; crave your anger
the angular sound of your birth; for my belief is in nothing

no fraternity with anything
my pedigree; my community is facile
I see the world through screens; through buffers
if I am somehow cork; you are the weather; the land
I wash up jetsam; on your shore
knock at your door
look at your faces; wonder what it would be like
to know all your names.

Bridges

JANICE JOHNSTON

I'm arranging my blanket on the cobbles when I hear the tap tap of shoes. I know it's her. She comes at the same time every morning. I turn to watch first her grey hair then her red coat appear over the brow of the bridge. She always looks smart and kind of elegant, I suppose, for an old woman. I guess she's about the same age as my granny will be now. Granny never looked like that though. She always wore jeans and flowery skirts, baggy jumpers and cheap T-shirts. You need money to look that elegant. Granny never had any spare cash, not with all of us to feed and buy clothes for, she always said.

The old woman's approaching me. With her grey hair and red coat and black bag and boots the only un-elegant thing is the Tesco's plastic bag clasped in her left hand. She's like one of those pictures – spot six deliberate mistakes, like dogs with three legs or no driver in a moving car - but the bag isn't a mistake. She's always carrying it in her hand every time I see her crossing the bridge. At first, I thought it didn't fit with her image but now I realise it is her image.

As she's about to pass me she turns and nods her head, ever so slightly. I flick my eyes and nod back. She's only started to respond to me these last few days. She's no do-gooder. She never speaks, never questions, only nods. She's nothing like

Granny. Granny always had to know everything. She'd question and pester and nag till she made me tell her far more than she needed to know.

I stand up to watch the woman turn at the end of the bridge and wait by the riverbank wall. The seagulls spot her first. With clamouring cries they circle, waiting. A pigeon hops along the lichen-covered sandstone to pause a fraction away from the bag. Still she waits. The salt smell of the sea envelops her.

Ducks clamber up the stone pier and quack impatiently. A pair of geese stretch their necks and honk. Finally, swans waddle across the mud. From the parapet I see white lines of birds twist from side to side, all pointing to the woman.

Now she reaches into the plastic bag and the clamouring, squawking, crying and honking becomes even louder as the birds fight for bread. Only the biggest birds in the biggest group – the swans – are silent. But every bird gets its fair share, she makes sure of this. She shakes the final crumbs from the plastic bag and the pigeons and seagulls swirl overhead. A pause to check that there's nothing more to come, then the birds go back to their own lives; pigeons to the rooftops, seagulls to the air, swans, geese and ducks back to the river in slow procession. The swans waddling purposefully to the water's edge, scooping a beakful of water then sliding, elegant as their benefactor once more, into the river.

Below the Auld Brig, the sea rules the river. It's low tide, the river water surges over exposed rocks, making its way under the new bridge to the harbour, to the bay, to Arran in the distance. Granny always talked of taking us to Arran. She never did. She was always working, or one of us would be causing trouble at school, or the weather would be too rough to travel. Some excuse or other would stop her piling us all into a bus to Ardrossan, then boat to Brodick, to run wild over Goatfell. She was all talk.

Above, an aeroplane drones, carrying its passengers off to some far more exotic destination.

I settle back on to my blanket, pulling it round my legs in an attempt to protect myself from the cold hard cobblestones of the bridge. I balance a battered cardboard coffee cup by my feet. I hope.

I hear the tap tap of shoes again and she appears – grey hair, red coat, elegant. She pauses at my feet and I look up.

She hands me another Tesco bag. 'Cheese and pickle,' she says. Three little words, that's all.

Jean Armour Speaks

Ann Burnett

He wisnae much use as a husband, mind.
Oh aye, he was a charmer,
ask any lassie for miles aboot,
see it in eyes o weans scattered aw roun.
But reliable, naw. A guid provider, naw.
Too fu o ideas an thochts an thinkin, no enough hard labour.
Left me wi a newborn an a debt to pay,
a book o verse an scribblins, sangs an bawdy lines
that entertained his cronies many a night
while I watched the weans
an stoked the flames o wrath an regret.
Too fu o radical thoughts that had the long finger pointin an
murmurins o treason an revolution,
too fu o lust an adulterous fornication
for the black coated kirk to stomach.
Often too fu.
No, no a guid husband as you'd cry it,
but whit a man.

Dear Diaries

ROWENA M LOVE

She huddled in the middle of the bed, surrounded by the diaries. They seemed to get bigger in her mind until they rose like a wall around her. They balanced the depression her slight body made in the mattress; she could feel herself sinking deeper until it felt like a well – or a grave.

Her clothes were as worn as the moth-eaten curtains that struggled to hold the winter sun at bay. Ladders striped her tights, revealing the fluorescent white flesh beneath. Her mascara had long since panda-ed her eyes to a mockery of Dusty Springfield.

'Why?' she muttered to herself, rocking gently. 'Why?'

She closed her eyes and opened them, hoping that everything would have changed. It hadn't.

She picked up one of the diaries, holding it between thumb and forefinger as if it would bite, then just as quickly dropped it. She tried again, picking another diary at random. This time she got as far as riffling the pages but the writing blurred before she could even make out the year. She rubbed once more at her eyes, these fresh tears and the mascara overflowing to make a cataract of black across her cheek.

'It's not fair!' she said, as she flung the diary across the room. It hit the far wall and bounced off a pile of CDs. They rattled to the floor, half-burying the red velvet-covered book.

Debbie scrabbled amongst the diaries on the bed, flinging them one after the other at the same wall, chanting 'No! No! No!' every time she did so. With a single sweep of her arm she shoved the ones that were left to the floor, then curled with foetal fervour into her sobs. A teddy bear on the pillow seemed to stare at her, its unblinking eyes hard and unsympathetic; it was a long time before the tears ran dry.

When they did, she lay still. Occasionally, she would make a sound that was half way between a sigh and a whimper.

She took a deep breath and sat up, slowly, for her very bones seemed to have aged. She slid off the bed onto the floor, then used the bed to help her to her knees. She rested her head on her folded arms at the edge of it for a moment, and then straightened her back. It had to be done.

Still on her knees, she shuffled between the diaries on the floor, picking them up and stacking them in a rough pile. Barbie pink screamed against lush velour, but Debbie didn't sort them, just kept adding them to the pile. It started to list drunkenly to one side.

'There'll be time enough to sort them,' she thought. 'Too much time.'

'It's all there,' Sharon had said. 'I've noted every bit of it down. Dates, times, I've got it all. Or rather, my Darling Diary does.' She'd laughed, her eyes sparkling in a strange combination of delight and malice. 'Guess who's going to be very, very rich?'

Sharon's voice echoed in the room, as did the laughter. Debbie whirled round, expecting to see Sharon at her shoulder, but there was no one there. The laughter died away, leaving just the mocking tick of the alarm clock that she'd given Sharon in a present years ago. The silver balls that rose on springs above its fluffy covering seemed to nod agreement: Sharon might have been very, very stupid rather than rich, but Debbie hadn't been an awful lot better.

It had seemed so simple – let Lennie know what Sharon was up to and she'd maybe get a chance of something nice. A lot of something, he'd be so grateful. Okay, so maybe she and Sharon had been best friends since before they could even write and Sharon first started keeping her stupid Darling Diary, but Sharon hadn't planned to share any of it with her, so why shouldn't Debbie have made her own arrangements?

Debbie's breath hitched, the tears threatening once more at the memory of Lennie's shouts: 'You get those diaries, you stupid little bitch. Or else!' No offer of some extra for her, no hint of a special deal, just a promise of his fists if she didn't sort Sharon out. In the meantime he wasn't giving her anything more.

She'd gone over to see Sharon, prepared to play nice and persuade her round to Debbie's point of view. She'd been doing that for years – Sharon always crumbled in the end.

'What do you want?' Sharon had said, not even opening the door properly to let her in.

'Aw come on, Shar, no need to be like that.'

'Look, Debbie, I'm knackered. I don't have time for one of your sessions.'

Debbie could see that Sharon must have had one of her all-nighters. That wasn't anything new. Put her in front of a computer and she completely lost track of time. 'Just a few minutes, Sharon. Please.' She tried the cajoling smile that had never failed to get Sharon doing what she wanted her to.

'Oh, all right. But not for long. This project isn't finished and I've a deadline coming up.' Sharon had opened the door and let her in.

'I thought you wouldn't need to work so hard with all this money you've got coming.'

'Yes, well, I won't get that just yet, so I need to carry on with my usual stuff while I'm waiting for the life of Riley.' Sharon went over to the windows to open the curtains and let in some light when Debbie said hesitantly: 'About that – there might be a slight problem.'

Sharon's hand on the old curtain slipped to her side as she whirled to confront Debbie. 'What do you mean?'

Debbie cleared her throat, then tried her usual smile.

Sharon just gave her a Paddington hard stare. 'Well?'

'I didn't mean to let it slip,' she'd told her – well, she wasn't going to own up that she was trying to make her own deal with Lennie, now was she?

'Lennie was livid. He says you're in real bother if you don't keep your mouth shut about his activities. You'd better hand over the diaries to me and I'll pass them on to Lennie. If you don't, you're dead meat.'

Sharon had just looked at her. 'I'm giving you nothing, Debbie. Not even the time of day after this.' She'd turned her back on her, as if Debbie was less than a slater scurrying across the floor. 'And talking of time,' she said, over her shoulder, as she went back to her computer, 'You can tell Lennie that he'll soon be doing some if he doesn't make it worth my while. Now get out.'

'I didn't mean to do it,' Debbie whined to herself. 'But she shouldn't have tried to keep it all for herself. Shouldn't have talked to me like that.'

Debbie very carefully picked up the pile of diaries. Even though there didn't seem to be anything in them apart from Sharon's pash for the guy up the road, and the one on Kyle Evans in third year, she reckoned she'd better take them to show Lennie he was in the clear. She'd gone through every one of them afterwards and there was nothing in them. Nothing. So much for Sharon's taunts that she'd kept detailed notes, that her Darling Diary was witness to it all.

She just as carefully avoided looking over to the other side of the room, where Sharon lay, the blood around her head congealing into a twisted halo.

'Wasn't my fault,' Debbie's list of excuses to herself, for herself, dribbled on. No reason why anyone should think it was anything but an accident – the rug tangled under Sharon's lifeless feet was evidence enough of how it happened. No one would know of the shove that started her fall, so Debbie would be in the clear. But she'd have the diaries, just in case there was some special code and the information about Lennie was in there after all.

'Even if they do check out fingerprints and stuff,' she thought, 'well we were mates, weren't we? Course they'll find mine in her room.'

The sharp edge of the computer monitor was smeared with blood – that's what had done the damage, after all, and Debbie's fingerprints wouldn't be anywhere near that as she couldn't stand the blasted things. Mobiles, yes, she'd had one surgically attached for years, but don't ask her to do any really technical stuff. Unlike Sharon, who'd lived for the things. 'Or died for the things,' Debbie sneered at the corpse in the corner.

Debbie never thought to tally up the diaries. She was in no fit state, either, to notice that the diaries in her hand only went up to when Sharon was about sixteen. Just around the time that she really got in to computers in a big way. But unlike the junkie in a fix, the police wouldn't fail to notice.

Intimates

DOUGLAS GRAY

We're all made out of light, open
to its properties with each analysis:
I'm thinking of the heat contained in an orange,

the aura's ember glow, a restless fruit
that flashes till the traffic lights are ripe;
a country boy of green, with fields

and hills of tress that stretch for miles,
where rough-and-ready jealousy resides,
lurking in the homelands of my heart.

It's fluffed and made of pretty, pink,
like cardigans that mother used to wear,
half-away to anger, but much too shy to say.

And who can treasure brown, nothing
but a stain on the emphasis of bright,
a slum in the plush of its brothers?

Or take to heart a relative of yellow,
with no real depth in skin that fades away,
60w of radiance towards a little thought?

So I come to white, absolute of neutral,
the virgin page that bleeds itself a tricolour of you:
black dress, blue room, red smile.

In the Gorbals

NORMAN BISSETT

Twa Glesca keelies,
wee Fenian guttersnipes,
bricht-eyed ragamuffins,

Tufted like waxwings,
inner-city sparras
wi' tackety bits

an' corrugatit socks
aroon their ankles,
Bert Hardy bairns

trailin' through canyons
o' grubby tenements,
dubs, dog shit.

Joan Eardley weans,
wi' cauliflower ears
an' latent strabismus,

aff-white knees,
breid-knife haircuts
an’ snottery ganseys

clutchin’ their bag,
their precious bawbees
an’ each ither

by the haun,
head aff chirpily
fir mammy’s messages,

milk, Mirror, Woodbines,
keechie wee rapscallions,
stampin’ the sivers,

like fallen angels
meanderin’ towards heaven,
intae the licht.

Knitting for Joyce

Ann Burnett

Ah'm knitting a cardigan for Joyce in a heather mixture double knitting wool and number 7 needles. It's quick to do and ah'm already on the first sleeve and nearly up to the armhole. Ah've done the back and the left and right fronts and ah only startit it a couple o' weeks ago. Ah showed her the pattern, buttons up the front to the neck and a collar, and she said she liked the style so ah bought the wool and got startit. Ah wanted it to be a Christmas present for her but she said to dae nae such thing and at least to let her gi' me the cost of the wool. The present could be the time ah've spent on it. But ye ken, when ye think of all she does for me, it's the least she deserves, so mebbe ah'll knit her a scarf and a hat to match as a surprise.

Ah look at the clock above the dresser again and then ah get up and go ben the room to check on the wan there on the mantelpiece. Aye, the wan in the kitchen is right, it definitely is weel past eleven and there's still nae sign of her. It's no like Joyce to be this late in coming in. She's usually here afore ten to clean oot the grate and get the fire goin' in here. It's cauld and I shiver as I go over tae the windae and look oot. No that there's onything to see, the smog is that thick and ye cannae tell if it's day or night, it's that dark. Sounds are aw muffled up like scarves roon yer neck. Ah watch a tram-caur gaun doon the street and it sounds like its wheels are covered in cotton wool, no rattly and screeching, as it roons the corner. There's scarce ony body aboot, save a man, aw happit up wi his heid doon, gaun up the street. A'body's stayin put the day. There's nae point in gaun oot when ye cannae see yer haun in front o' ye. Even in the room it seems like there's wisps o' the fog driftin by, seepin in through the window frames and doon the lum.

It's quiet and ah can hear the clock tick, ticking away. The fire lies deid and the ashes are needin scraped oot. Joyce aye does it for me and fills the coal scuttle as ma knees urnae up tae bendin doon tae the hearth. Ah manage the kitchen range fine as it's no low doon and the bunker is right there but ah cannae manage the room fire and ah like it lit by eleven so's ah can go in there and sit in an afternoon. Whit's the point o' havin' a room and kitchen if ye dinnae use the room? Ah like tae sit in there o' an evening and listen tae the radio while ah knit. Ah like the Scottish dance music wi Jimmy Shand at half past six on the Scottish Home Service and after that there's maybe a play or a variety show so that before ah ken it, it's time tae pit ma needles away and gang ben the kitchen and get ready for ma bed. It's aye warm in there in the box bed as ah keep the range gaun aw night so's ah can have ma cuppa tea in the morning.

But Joyce hasnae been in yet and I stert tae wunner whit's happened. Maybe she didnae get hame frae her work last night if the smog was bad. She works in a pub in Argyle Street and usually disnae get back till after eleven by the time they've cleared up. Ah cannae see the attraction o' sitting in a pub till ten o'clock at night though Joyce says they get quite a few women in the lounge bar. It wisnae the done thing in ma day to go onywhere near a public hoose but things are changing that fast noo. Joyce says they're gonnae get a juke box pit intae the lounge bar so's you can put money in and pick a gramophone record to play. Anither thing apart from the beer to waste yer money on.

Ah straighten wan o' ma antimacassars oan the back o' the armchair. Ah mind when ah sewed it for ma bottom drawer and it looks aw right despite being past forty year auld. Though

Joyce says they're oot o' fashion noo but then whit does an auld buddy like me care whether ah'm in fashion or no? Ah go back ben the kitchen and take up ma knitting again. Maybe Joyce has had to stay the night wi a freen' if the buses werny runnin'. But the trams urny aff, they can aye run in the smog as they can jist keep tae the rails.

Ah measure the knitting against the inch chart on the edge of the pattern. Anither twa rows should dae it and then ah'll start takin in for the armhole. It's just plain knitting, nae fancy stitches or cables as ah think ye didnae see the heather effect o' the wool properly if you've got aw they fancy bits. So ah just purl away tae masel for the next couple o' rows.

It's been that guid havin' Joyce across the landing. She moved in aboot a year ago and we've been freens since even tho' she's in her twenties. She's that helpful and a guid laugh. I mind when she came in tae dae ma hair wi' wan o' they new home perms. Whit a time we had. It was a Sunday and we talked the whole time she wis pittin' in the curlers and rinsing ma hair. A freen had done hers the week afore and ah fair admired it so Joyce said she wid dae mine fur me. Ah'd made some scones for when we had tae sit and wait for the lotion tae take. When Joyce had finished she held up the mirror so's ah could see masel and then jouked doon so's she wis next tae me and said, 'Which twin has the Toni?' We laughed till the tears wis runnin' doon ma face. There ah wis wi aw ma wrinkles and her wi her rosy cheeks and bonnie blue eyes and looking naethin like twins. Whit a laugh it wis.

Ah look up at the clock again and it's getting later. She's maybe havin a long lie though it's no like her, she's ay up and busy. She's even startit knitting. Ah couldnae believe her when she said she couldnae knit. Whit did they teach ye at yer school? ah says. Did aw wee lassies no get learnt how tae knit? But she said she wis aw butterfingers and the teacher aye belted her fur drapping the stitches and so she never learnt. Ah rummled aboot in ma knitting bag and gied her some left over green double knitting and a pair o' size 8's. Ah keep ma needles aw thegither in anither bag, aw tied up in twos wi a wee bit o the wool ah last used them tae knit something wi. The size 8's had been a jumper for ma nephew in a dark broon which ah think he likes. It's never aff his back ony how.

Anyway, ah casted on twenty stitches for Joyce and did the first row, jist plain, tae get her startit. Then ah showed her, in, over, through and aff, in, over, through and aff, but she wis right aboot the butterfingers, mair ham-fisted like. Ah never saw a lassie sae awkward wi her needles but she said she wanted tae learn and did ah no have ony finer needles? Ah tellt her tae stick wi' the big wans though they were that plastic stuff and no ma guid Aero needles. Ah dinnae want tae loss ony o' them but ah dinnae tell her that, ah dinnae want tae hurt her feelings when she's that nice tae me.

Ah cannae settle tae ma knitting so ah hae a rummle in ma bag an that's when ah spot that wan o' ma number 13's must have slipped oot its wool as there's only the wan there. It's a right fine needle that 13, and ah use them for shawls fur the weans. Then ah get that sair feeling in ma hert even though it's near forty year ago. Ah'd knitted a bonny white shawl for him, aw scalloped edges and fanshells an ah wrapped it roon him so he wis aw happit up and pit him in his wee box which wis aw we had tae bury him in. 'That's a right waste,' ma man said, 'burying him in a brand new shawl scarce used' but ah knew ah widnae be needin it again and onyway ah wanted him tae know his mammy cared for him and ah wanted him tae be warm though ah kent he widnae be warm ever again.

Ah feel a tear beginning tae creep intae ma een so ah get up and pu' the kettle over the fire and ah tak oot a cup and saucer and the tin wi' ma pancakes in that ah made for Joyce yesterday. She wisnae feelin herself and didnae hae wan. Ah wunner if she's all right – she's no been herself lately, a bit peely-wally and wi' nae appetite tae speak of. The pancakes are a wee bit hard noo, they're aye better fresh but ah pit them back in the tin because ah'm wonderin if maybe Joyce is no weel and in her bed. The mair ah think on it, the mair ah realise that she's no been that great fur a wee while. Kin' o' pale and doon and … distracted.

Ah'm staunin there wondering whit tae dae when ah sees her key hingin on the dresser. Ah made her gie me it efter she wis locked oot the wance and hud tae get a man tae break the lock fur her. So ah said ah'd keep a spare key if she didnae mind and it's jist as well as she's had tae borrow it mair than wance. Ah'm wonderin if ah should gie her door a wee chap jist tae check she's ok. Ah'm no wantin tae be nosy like but it's gone twelve the noo and she's no been in.

Ah take the key aff its hook and open ma door. The smog's got in tae the close and it's swirlin aboot like wraiths on the landing. It's quiet, no a soun', and ah hear ma ain feet shuffle ower tae her door. Ah gie it a wee chap and then anither but there's nae answer. Ah pause before ah pit the key in the lock, ah dinnae want her tae think ah'm spying on her or onything like that but ah ken ah'm worrit. Ah open the door a keek and call 'Joyce' but she disnae reply. Ah call again and push the door a wee bit wider and that's when ah think she must hae bought new linoleum as it's no the usual green, it's darker. But then something makes me go in and ah see that it's no new linoleum, it's the flair's that's wet and sticky wi' dark stuff. Ma hert starts loupin' and ah push open her kitchen door and she's lying there on the flair and there's towels and sheets aw aboot her and they're aw stained, stained deep dark red and her face is that white and her rosy cheeks is aw gone and her eyes, her bonnie blue eyes are closed and ah ken she's deid.

'Joyce,' ah hear masel saying but ah ken it's nae use, 'Joyce.' Ah ken whit's happened, whit she's done, pair lassie, and that's when ah see it lying there on the flair in amang aw the blood, but still shiny and sharp. Ma number 13 Aero knitting needle.

The Ben

ROWENA M LOVE

Pine tree hackles rise
on the back of the Ben
that crouches dog-like
in the mists of morning.

Shadows brindle its coat
where it's matted with heather,
or brushed the wrong way
by the ice age's careless hand.

Beneath its chin, a collar of cliffs,
the frill of a waterfall;
wind in a clump of birches
sets a happy tail wagging.

Other

Duncan Fraser

Absurd, really, the moves of the mating game,
trying not to reveal your desperate desire for love,
cold feet alternating with sudden boldness,
being concussed by the apples of erotic gravity,
waking up to the discovery that you're
a paper clip attached to a horseshoe magnet.
But the craving for intimacy is so strong,
burning as hot as sunlight,
turning you into a nuclear fireball
continually on the sniff for a companion star.
Come on sweetheart, you know
you want to form a binary system.
Love, the star turn, can, however,
suddenly and so easily cease to exist.
A parallel universe can materialise
in which everything is reversed.
Light becomes dark,
silence replaces dialogue,
commitment turns into apathy.

A lover with no further use for you
will chuck you out.
Even in Cloud Cuckoo Land
they are constrained
by the exigencies of realpolitik.
So what is left?
Well, there is feeling sorry for yourself,
but also for those you have hurt,
and, strangely, even for those
you have been hurt by.
There is a longing for significance,
a longing that points towards something
on the periphery, an unobtrusive,
all-embracing compassion
at the edge of experience,
something in the background,
like the background radiation
of the Universe, detectable everywhere,
but generally overlooked.
God's late style.

Ayr Writers' Club

SHEILA GRANT

Ayr Writers' Club was formed by Elsie Miller in 1970 and has since grown to become one of the biggest writing groups in Scotland. In over thirty years, the club has helped many members achieve publication. The syllabus is designed to nurture the tiniest gem of an idea and turn it into an article, story, poem, or performance piece. Workshops in poetry, drama, fiction, non-fiction and writing for children are held on a monthly basis and led by experienced writers.

Well known writers and authors visit the club every month to speak and adjudicate. Recent speakers have included Janice Galloway, Des Dillon, Jenny Colgan, Mairi Hedderwick, Aileen Paterson, Ian Rankin and Hugh Rae, who writes as Jessica Stirling, Margaret Thomson Davis, Denise Mina, Joyce Holms, Maggie Craig, Evelyn Hood, Catherine Czerkawska, Marc Pye and Alex Gray.

The club meets every Wednesday night from September to June in Kyle Academy, Ayr and welcomes all aspiring writers from total beginners to those who have already experienced success. The aim of the club is to see the members achieve publication. The success can range from a letter to the local paper to a blockbuster novel. On average, more than twenty members achieve publication in any one year in poetry, articles, fiction, children's writing, drama, radio and television. These successes can be multiplied still further by the number of items published by each member.

Most people join with a fixed idea of the genre they want to write. The workshops run by the club give members a chance to try all the genres and more than one member has discovered to their delight that they have a particular flair for something quite unexpected. There are a number of writing competitions throughout the year with trophies and book tokens as prizes.

Through the years, the members of Ayr Writers' Club have written for a wide range of publications including The Herald, Evening Times, The Scotsman, Scots Magazine, Scottish Field, Reader`s Digest, Sunday Times, Daily Express and many other regional newspapers. Women's magazines that have published a short story, feature or filler include Woman, Woman's Own, Yes magazine, The Lady, Bella, Best, Woman's Weekly, My Weekly and the People's Friend. Members have also scripted work for Radio Scotland and Radio Ulster.

In 1996, an anthology of work done by members over the years was published to coincide with the Burns Bi-centenary and the club's silver jubilee. Members take part in the annual *Burns an' a' that* Festival, giving readings throughout Ayrshire.

New members are always welcome, whether they are complete beginners or have already achieved publication. See **www.ayrwritersclub.co.uk** for further details.

Biographies

Fiona Atchison joined Ayr Writers' Club in 2004. She combines a fulltime job with writing for pleasure. Fiona won the Dorothy Dunbar Trophy for poetry at The Scottish Association of Writers' Conference in 2005. Crime writing is a genre she enjoys and has won the AWC Crime Story competition two years in a row. Now aged 46, it is her future ambition to work part-time and devote more time to writing.

Kate Ayres I was born in South Wales but lived abroad for a good part of my childhood, returning to Wales to sit O-levels. I have three children, decided to start a BA (Hons) English last year, and while I enjoyed the course, I have now changed to script writing. I was inspired to write the story following a lecture when we discussed how our individual histories influence how we write. I was intrigued about an event I had grown up knowing but had no actual recollection of myself. *The Cry* is the true story of my birth and the best compliment for it I could have had is the fact that both my parents cried when they read it!

Norman Bissett worked for the British Council, 1964-95, in Lebanon, Turkey, Uruguay, Spain, Scotland, Egypt and the Philippines. President, Edinburgh Writers' Club for the past 3 years. Since retiring in 1995 he has had many poems published in the small press. A frequent Quantum Leap competition prize-winner, he is also a past winner of The Scottish International Poetry Competition and of open competitions organised by Partners, Writing Magazine, The Literary Review and Edinburgh City Council. His first collection, *Following the Wagons*, is due to be published later this year.

Debby Broughton-Hay I'm originally from the Yorkshire/Lancashire area. My first writing experience was creating a children's history book about my hometown Barnoldswick. Following University I started writing seriously, mainly short stories and drama, although like most writers I've also started a novel. I joined Ayr Writers Club in 1999 and am proud to be President this year.

Ann Burnett writes scripts for BBC children's radio and television programmes as well as publishing articles and short stories. She joined Ayr Writers' Club in 1979 when her first son was a year old and learned all she knows from the speakers' nights and workshops she attended. At present she is studying for an M.Litt in Creative Writing at Glasgow University and working on a novel.

Sylvia Cohen I have always loved works of the imagination and read voraciously. My desire to write though got lost in having to weave an intricate path through the demands of children and work. Since life has become somewhat less complex, I am re-visiting creative writing – and enjoying it.

Des Dillon was born in Coatbridge, Lanarkshire, Scotland, in 1960, and read English at Strathclyde University. A former teacher, he now writes for television, stage and radio and has taught Creative Writing at the Arvon Foundation. He was Writer in Residence at Castlemilk, Glasgow, between 1998 and 2000, and now lives in Galloway. He has written seven novels, including *Me and Ma Gal* (1995), *Duck* (1998), *Itchycooblue* (1999), and *The Big Q* (2001). *Six Black Candles* (2002), was originally written as a play in 1999 and was premiered at The Royal Lyceum Theatre in Edinburgh in Spring 2004.

Duncan Fraser was born in Inverness and went to Stirling University. His poems have appeared in First Time, Other Poetry, and Pulsar. He has recently won the Colloquy Poetry Competition. He lives in Perth.

Sheila A. Grant I joined Ayr Writers' Club intending to write for children. After success in a club competition I began concentrating on non-fiction. I have been published in the local and national press and in several women's magazines. I review books, primarily for newBooks magazine. Last year I was a judge for the Foster Grant Romantic Novel of the Year prize.

Douglas W Gray is 47 years old and lives in Cove Bay, Aberdeen. He is a founder member of the Dead Good Poets, a charity poetry reading group who meet on the last Thursday of each month, with guest readers and open mic. Published widely in the small press circuit and a former editor of two poetry magazines, Storm and Spume. He was second in Northwords Poetry Competition 1998, won first prize in the Feile Filiochta and the Irish Times Perpetual Trophy 2001, and second again in the Scottish International Poetry Competition 2003. A forthcoming publication *Flesh, Place and Other Colours* is due out in early 2006.

Joanne Harris was born in 1964 to a French mother and an English father. After Cambridge, she taught for fifteen years and published three novels, one of which, *Chocolat*, was filmed starring Juliette Binoche and Johnny Depp. Since then, she has written five more novels, *Blackberry Wine, Five Quarters of the Orange, Coastliners, Holy Fools* and *Gentlemen and Players*. She has also written *Jigs and Reels*, a collection of short stories, and two cookbooks. In 2005 she judged the Orange prize.

Jim Hughes was born in Ayrshire and followed the West of Scotland tradition of engineering, which led him into a successful career as a manager, industrialist, and University professor. The main theme of his many tasks and challenges in his work has been the behaviour, conflict and growth of individuals in the complex and frustrating context of work. In his attempt to make sense of, and contribute something new to the many paradoxes he encountered, he sought, and continues to seek, clues in the fields of psychology and spirituality. His writing, both prose and poetry, attempts to share some of these insights. He is one of the Makar Poets.

Janice Johnston started writing in the late 1990's and had her first success, a children's story, published in My Weekly in 1999. Since then she has had a number of children's stories, scripts for BBC Radio Ulster and BBC TV, humorous articles, non-fiction and women's fiction published both here and abroad.

Rowena M Love, another Makar poet, is based in Troon, in the West of Scotland. She started writing seriously in 1997 and since then has racked up many successes. She has had hundreds of poems published in a wide variety of places and has done well in competitions, too. She also writes non-fiction, with many articles to her credit. You can find out more about Rowena, and see further samples of her work on her website: **www.rowenamlove.co.uk**. Rowena is Writer in Residence for Ayrshire charity Writability and is on the Live Literature Scotland database.

Maya Rae MacLaughlin I have been writing for most of my life so I am very happy to have one of my short stories selected as a prize-winner in the Ayr 800 Writing Competition. My portfolio of work is extensive including shorts, poetry and full-length works so I am delighted to add the success of *Obeahman* to my résumé. My agent is also delighted! As with most writers my ultimate goal is to see the publication of my novels. Recognition serves to spur the writer on to more success and for this I am grateful.

Michael Malone hails from Ayrshire, most of which he has covered in his various guises as Financial Adviser, Bookseller, Life Coach, Creative Writing Lecturer and Poet. Since he began writing he has been widely published in literary magazines and anthologies, including a spell as the Scottish Correspondent for Writers' Forum. Through his many successes, one of his greatest pleasures has been working with the other Makar Press poets as they spread the word on poetry the length and breadth of the country.

Marion Montgomery was born in Edinburgh in 1932. As an evacuee, she attended four primary schools and one secondary (Dundee High), then St.Andrews M.A. before returning to Edinburgh for Dip.Ed and marriage. She taught English in Fife, Warwickshire and Strathclyde and is now a WEA tutor living in Kilmarnock. Member of Ayr Writers' Club since 1974. Poetry published in the Herald, Scots Magazine, New Writing Scotland and Poetry Scotland.

Marion Reid From 'Farm Gate' to 'The Towering Wallace', Marian has had many poems published; also articles, children's stories and letters. A founder member of Ayr Writers' Club, she edited their anthology *Honest Men and Bonnie Lassies* in 1996. American by birth, Scottish by residence, she now has official dual nationality.

Knotbrook Taylor I have been writing poetry for 15 years now and during that time have performed at the Edinburgh Fringe, the Shore Poets and most recently the Wordplay Festival on Shetland. I have been published in various literary magazines including Northwords, Storm, Spume, Pushing out the Boat, and Cutting Teeth. My poetry comes from a deep-seated need to express myself. I never know what is going to trigger the next poem. It could be a dream, a feeling or a phrase someone says to me; whatever it is, poetry is something I need to do to keep a creative dimension to my life.

Sheila Templeton was born in Aberdeen, then spent an itinerant childhood ranging from Rannoch Moor to Dar-es-Salaam and back to Aberdeenshire. Though she left her roots forty years ago, her work still draws on that rich Buchan landscape. She now lives right by the sea in Ayrshire which still feels like dancing at a surprise party. The beach dancing led to a first poetry collection as a Makar Poet, *Slow Road Home*, as well as publication in many magazines, anthologies and readings on Radio Scotland. She has also been successful in several national poetry competitions. In addition to poetry, Sheila writes fiction for adults and children. She is currently trying to learn the Argentine Tango.

Dr E. J. Yeaman I'm a former Chemistry teacher. When I retired (escaped, early), I realised I would now have time to write something more interesting than lesson notes, summaries and exams. I joined Angus Writers' Circle, and the one at Dundee College. Having heard my work, members suggested, 'You should write for children.' I took that as a compliment, and that has been my main occupation since, although publishers have so far failed to share my enthusiasm for the stories. I've always believed, as the butler suggests in *Verdant Boughs at Twilight*, that, 'As long as at least one copy of [a] novel exists, and as long as there is someone to read it, then [its characters] live – live in a reader's imagination.' Thence the story.